REZI
VAN
LANKVELD

REZI VAN LANKVELD

AT THE FIRST CLEAR SIGHT

RIDINGHOUSE

CONTENTS
INHOUD

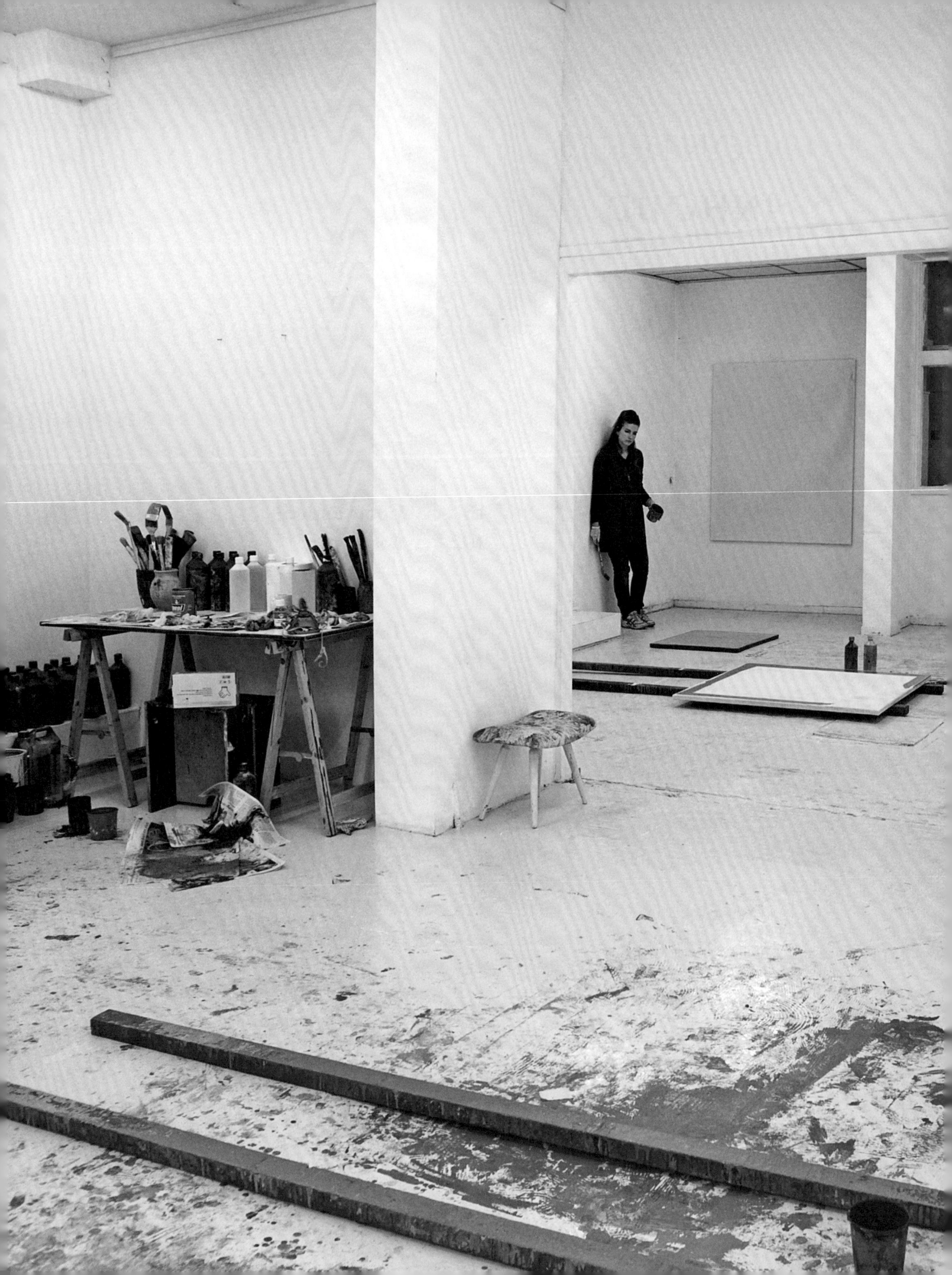

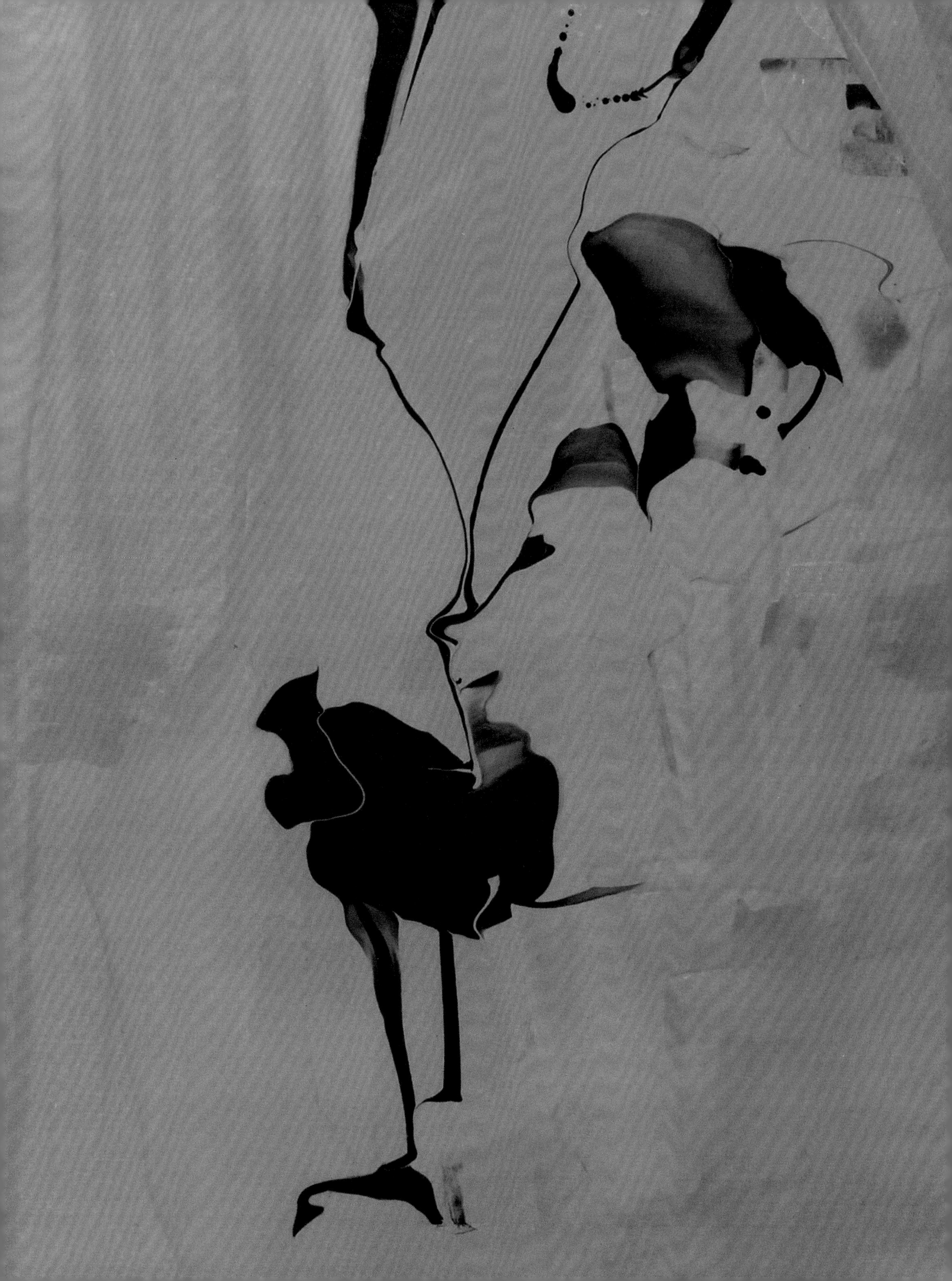

2009
SPIRIT
160 x 132 cm

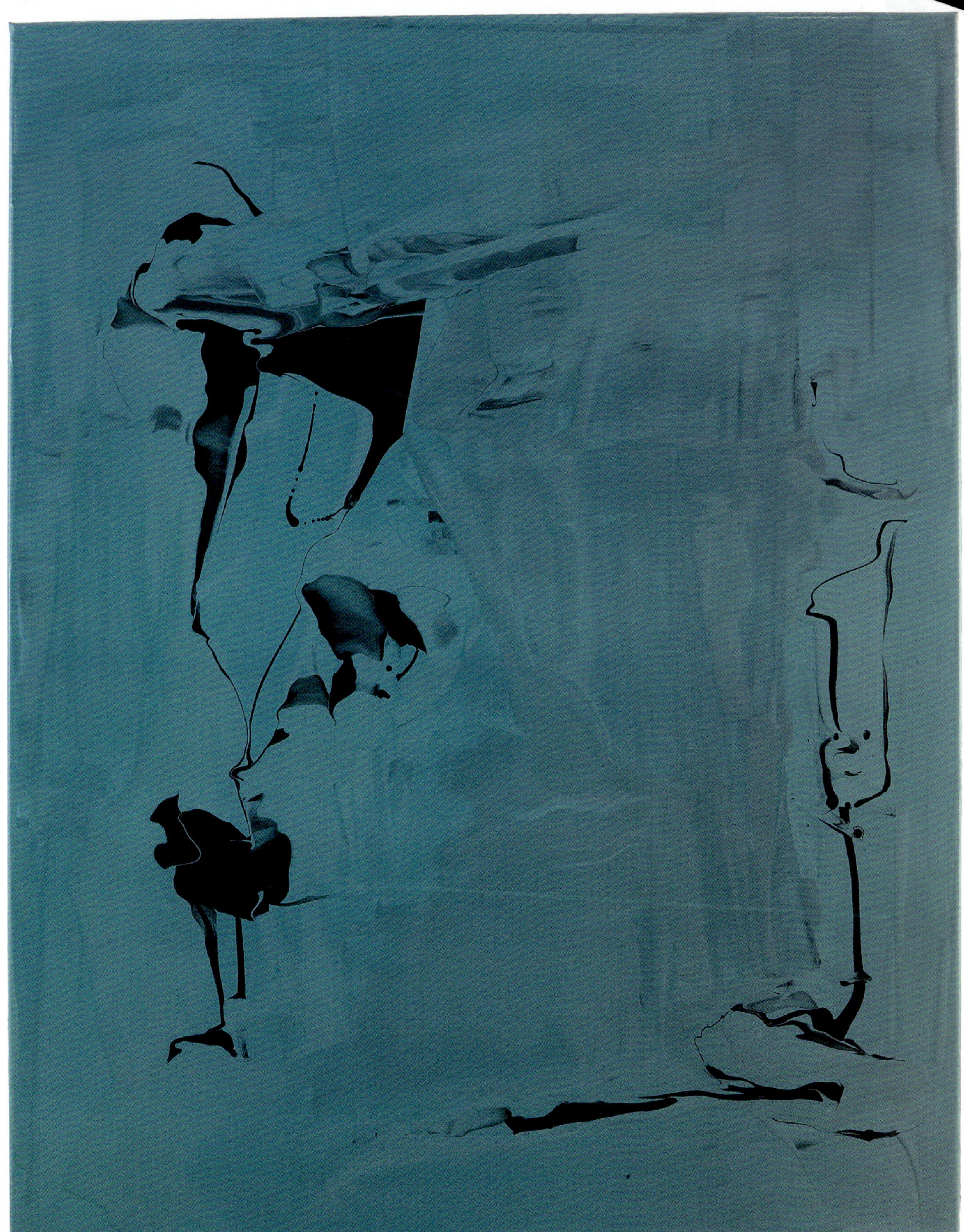

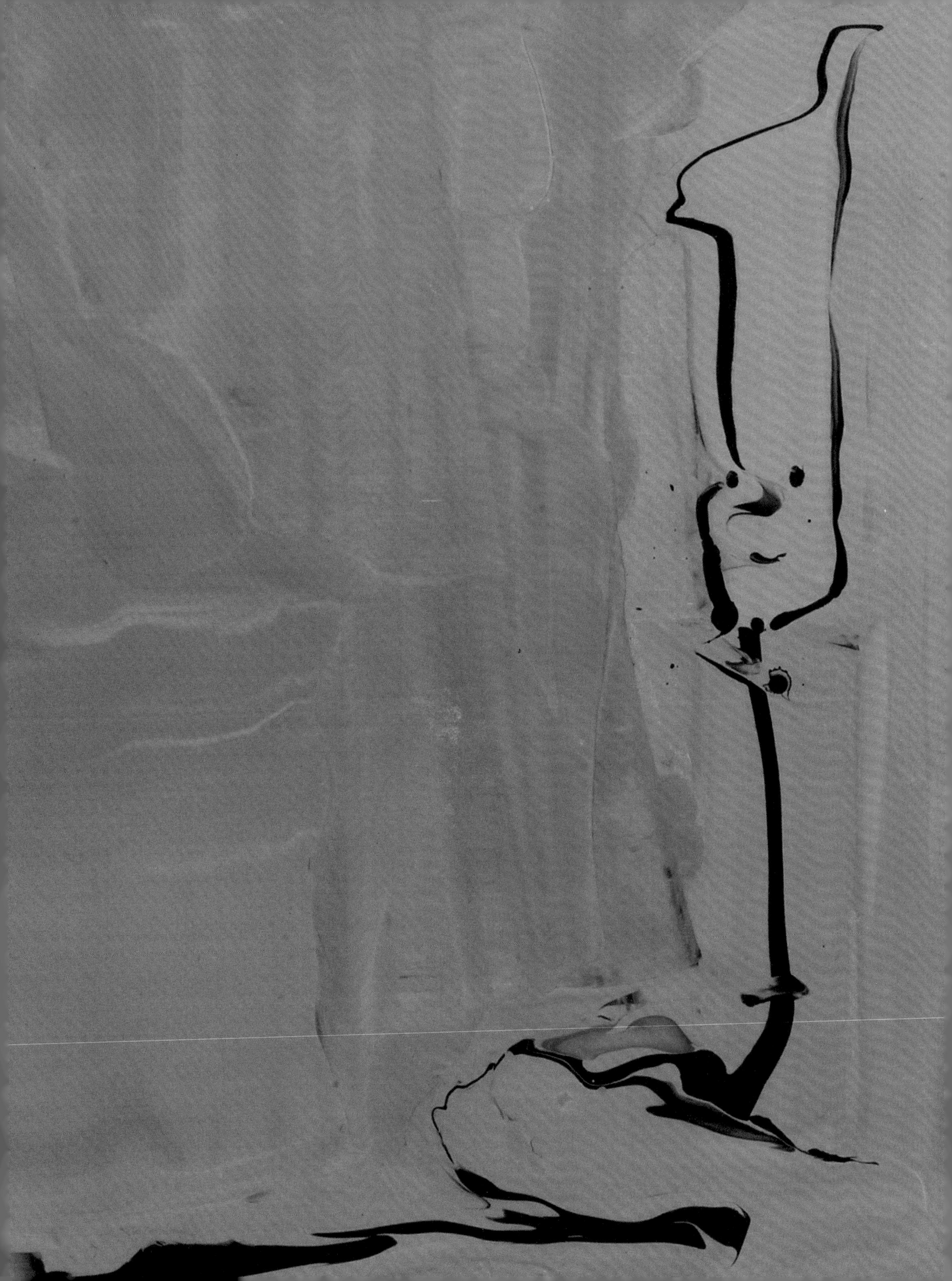

COME UNDONE
ZLATKO WURZBERG

page 12
SPIRIT
(detail, see page 11)

More often than not, a painting will be discussed in terms of its model, of what it refers to and the context in which it appears. A work of art references either some prior model or its own subsequent viewer, as if it were a transparent medium, an intermediary between those opposite issues. While contemplating historical or contemporary works of art featuring any degree of figuration, we still assume the depicted figures precede the paintings – which are considered to be their images – as if this habit has never been undermined by the experience of abstract art. For centuries, we tended to see a work of art as a reflection or a representation of the world. What mattered above all was the content, the details and the meaning of the depicted action, as well as the artist's skillfulness in expressing ideas. It had been assumed that the inception of any work of art is based on some kind of content (such as a motive or an idea), set beforehand as the origin of an action or a future work.

Over the lengthy period of Modernism, however, painting veered towards self-referentiality. Just like other arts, painting had set out to lay claim to a specific area of competence, where it was to focus on reflecting itself in a sort of intransitiveness and further develop this quality. This notion was conclusively formulated by the American critic Clement Greenberg: "The essence of Modernism lies, as I see it, in the use of characteristic methods of a discipline to criticise the discipline itself, not in order to subvert it but in order to entrench it more firmly in its area of competence."

Painting has subsequently reverted back to reflecting the outside world. Yet, it now endeavors to represent other representations of the world, ranging from symbolic and photographic to cinematic and journalistic and beyond. It has established itself as an art medium without tradition or, at best, as homage to mastership (this idea can, indeed, be dated back to Edouard Manet).

On the other hand, one might point out that abstract art presupposes an initial act of self-establishment and self-creation. It postulates that this act is both the inception (in the sense that nothing precedes it) and the selfsame spark that incites it. Consequently, this motive force is the initial artistic gesture triggering all the processes which bring the work about. Rather than being a mere executor, it is directly transposed into the work, indistinguishable from what it creates. This creation is, in turn, identical with the gesture itself. Instead of presenting itself as a confluence of various sources that find their expression within the work, it has one single author. The artistic subject creates from within itself and is the very origin of the work. The painted image does not owe itself to anything else.

Rezi van Lankveld's painting sets about making the image an exclusively pictorial event. The image must be a clear expression of its genesis: it emerges within the process of its own formation, as a projection of the painter's inner world seen with her mind's eye. Without reflecting anything extrinsic, it opens onto an imaginary world. Never arbitrary, the realm of Van Lankveld's imagination is deeply motivated by the logic of her painting method. It is clear from the outset that Rezi van Lankveld has no intention of either depicting a world – be it real or fantastic – or illustrating an idea. This can be inferred from her rejecting all pictorial illusion and any hint of realistic representation which might presume some kind of painterly illusionism. The painting as such must first reveal itself in its materiality, laid bare as color and paint, layer and stroke, as their movement on the surface etc. It must be capable of creating its own world. Although those paintings may recall "images made by chance" (as in Leonardo's example of decaying walls or Alexander Cozens's blot painting), they have been produced with great deliberation. From the very beginning, the painter strives towards an image: she sets out to produce an image which is in itself an integral part of the working process and has no initial model that is to be transformed, subdued and eventually negated by the painting. The visual components produced by the process of painting do not add up to any kind of final whole. The image exists on the same level as all other material elements, intertwined in the ambiguity of form. Here, however, one does not detect the usual antithesis reducing the image either to pure forms, as if it were an abstraction, or to a figurative representation. Thus, one's gaze need not choose whether to look at the image or at the painting. Within the space of such a work, the gaze does not move to and fro between the bare manifestation of the art of painting on the one hand and its figures on the other, as if the two viewings hovered in juxtaposition. In other words, those paintings would not be interpreted in terms of Richard Wollheim's thesis of twofoldness of seeing-in and the simultaneous awareness of what has been depicted and of depiction, of the subject and the medium. Furthermore, a "seeing-in" viewing, as epitomised by the duck-rabbit image, does not apply either. There is constant awareness that one is looking at a painting: one is never under the illusion of viewing something akin to a depiction. The viewing of the painting is singular and this is where the imaginative experience comes from. The painting draws its force from the tension between the act of painting and the image, which can be said to be its content, but only in part. Image is not set against matter: their relationship is dynamic. It takes place within a space where everything can interact with everything else, or become anything else. Those images might refer to pop-culture or the history of art, to private motives and states or ephemeral situations. Their very heterogeneity might tempt one to perceive them – erroneously – as metapictures demonstrating the essence of the painting, or a particular attitude towards visuality itself: the image would thus appear as a reflection on the painting that produced it. The pictorial image is neither the content of painting nor painting as content: it is their go-between, the very act of transition and the point where unstable figures take shape in the never-ending knit between the viewer's imagination and the reality of the painting.

Van Lankveld paints in constant uncertainty where each gesture of the painter involves a new decision. If painting should be perceived as constant decision making, this is undoubtedly due to the variety of directions it may take in accordance with the existing points of reference within a particular painting – as well as to the fact that none of these directions is *a priori* the one of choice. The given points of reference come as consequences of painting rather than from the sensory stimuli of the outside world. No decision is imperative, as the choice to be made is never suggested and most certainly not prescribed – but it is this very freedom of choice that makes it necessary. Not making a choice means giving up on the image. Erroneous or unsatisfactory choices result in unconvincing paintings the artist will efface – and the painting game starts all over again. It is almost as if Van Lankveld wasn't painting, as if she was hastily silhouetting shapes in wet paint glaze, improvising their outlines. In fact, she never paints an image: rather, she anticipates it, like a voyeur waiting in ambush, hoping to see a coveted scene. It is less important to see something than to make believe something can be seen.

The medium in which Van Lankveld paints is liquid but volatile and does not allow for long pauses in the process. A session needs to be completed without a break. The artist uses her brush to model painterly forms in a wet layer of paint. However, instead of the impastoed quality of oil or acrylic paint, the surface of the painting has a fresco-like dryness. The same applies to the colors: not only are their shades homogeneous, but they arc also toned down and muted, leaning towards grisaille in stark contrast to primary colors. Shades overlap, ooze over the surface, spread freely or are directed by the brush in a fluid matter reminiscent of gouache. Most of the surface is either partially or completely covered in paint. The stroke – in turns constructive and descriptive or nervous and shaky, but invariably light – never defines a complete form. Never whole, just partial or merely hinted at, the shapes create a surface in rhythmic movement. The painting finds its dynamic equilibrium in the image: the image is the point of reference the eye of the viewer can rely on, and from where the work derives its essence. As for their composition, most paintings display an undulating, circular rhythm, similar to ripples on water after tossing a stone. (Esthetically, the closest correspondent in traditional painting would be a floating drapery. In classical theories of painting, the beauty of a drapery was a gray area where technical rules of painting were found lacking, where they fell short or proved to be void – and yet the task required consummate skill. Such an impression of movement provided the painting with a temporal dimension which dramatised it and gave it an illusion of life.)

In this survey of Van Lankveld's work, one might be tempted to see an evolution in the shaping of images, from a scene where one might discern several figures, a spectacle of sorts, to a figurative indication of an attitude, an expression or an emotional state such as a curious gaze or indifference – a specific contour of people, things, landscapes and so on.

Here, the image reveals itself as a knot, a sketch, a blur. The artist prefers to show it as a knot rather than to clarify and elaborate it until all ambiguity is dispelled and we can understand it better. This knot is a hybrid body, a mash-up of acquired practices, models and observations. Nothing in these paintings feels transparent or innocent, neutral or whole – either on the level of what has been painted or on the level of the image. This might bring to mind Milan Kundera's image of "magic curtain hung before the world", as a ready-made pre-conception, a pre-interpretation of the world it veils. The aim of literature, he argues, is not to mistake the curtain for the world behind it, but to rip through the curtain and reveal the world in its nakedness. Consequently, could not the images of set postures, recycled symbols and other figures observed in Van Lankveld's paintings be perceived as copies of those fables woven in the curtain of pre-interpretation? They might – providing that in doing so one also sees them as a shape identical to the rip itself.

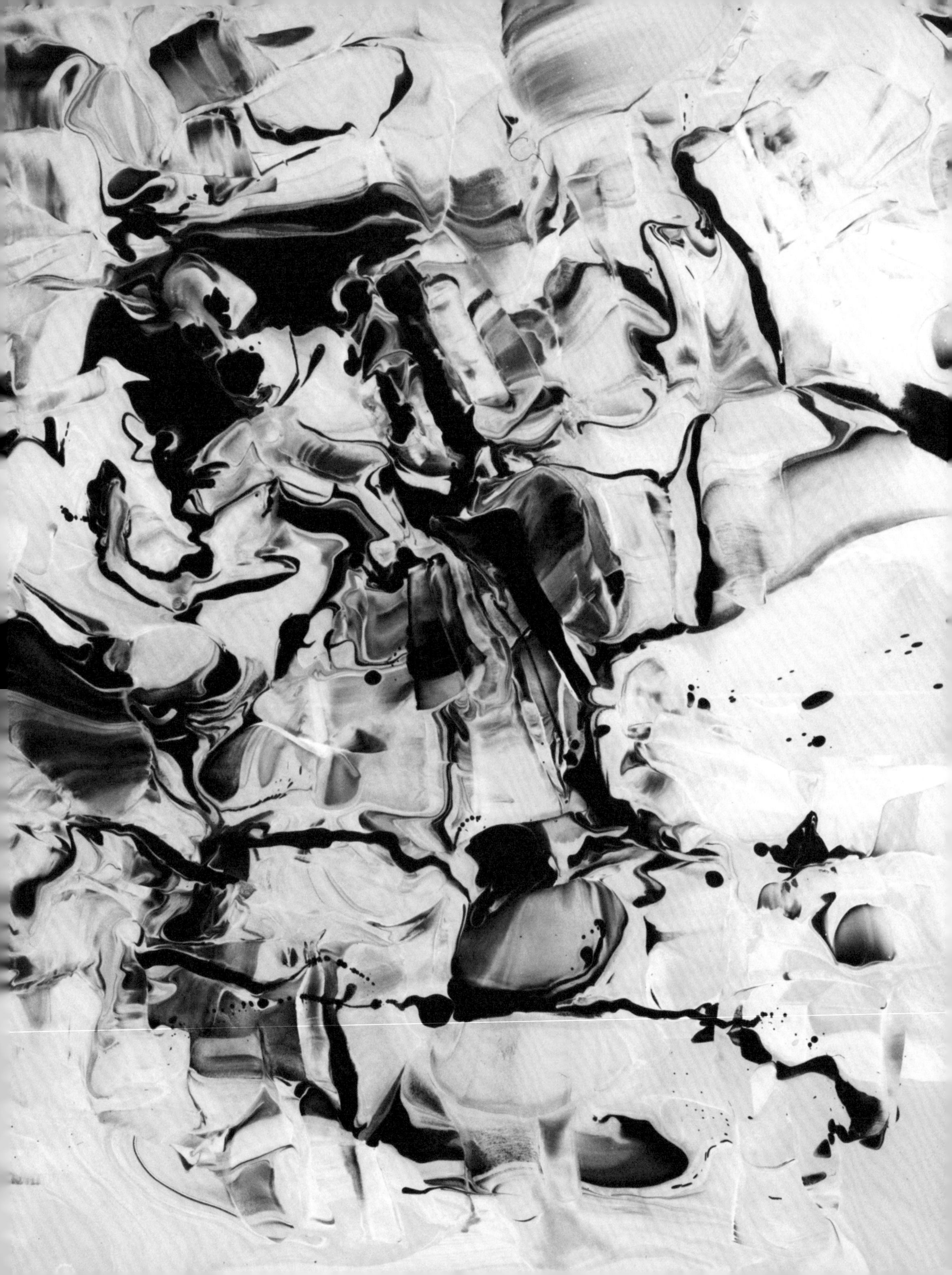

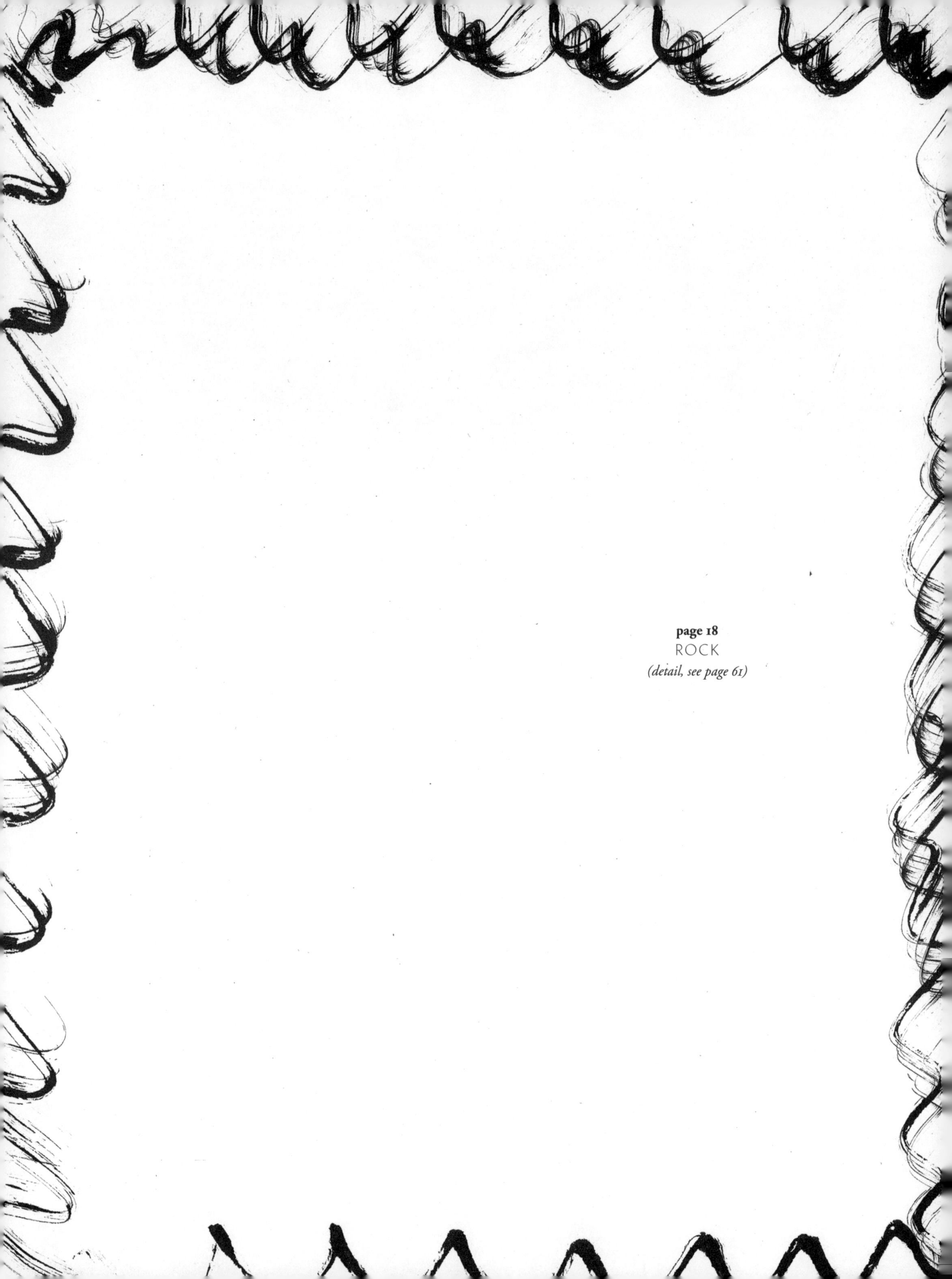

page 18
ROCK
(detail, see page 61)

2003
UNTITLED
27 x 31 cm

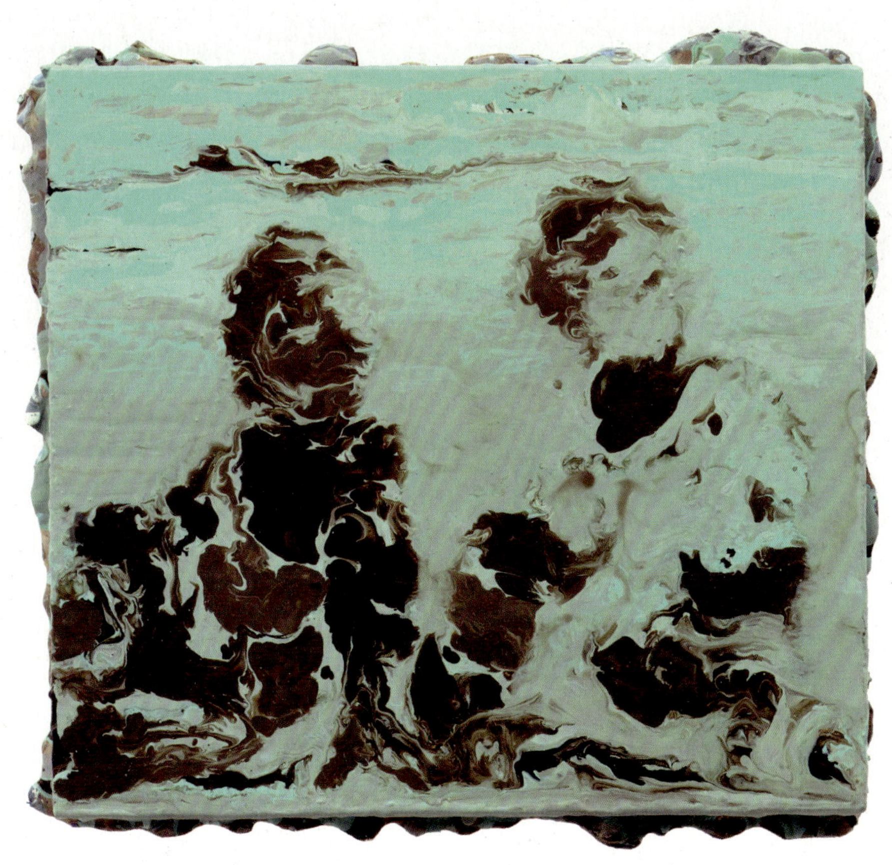

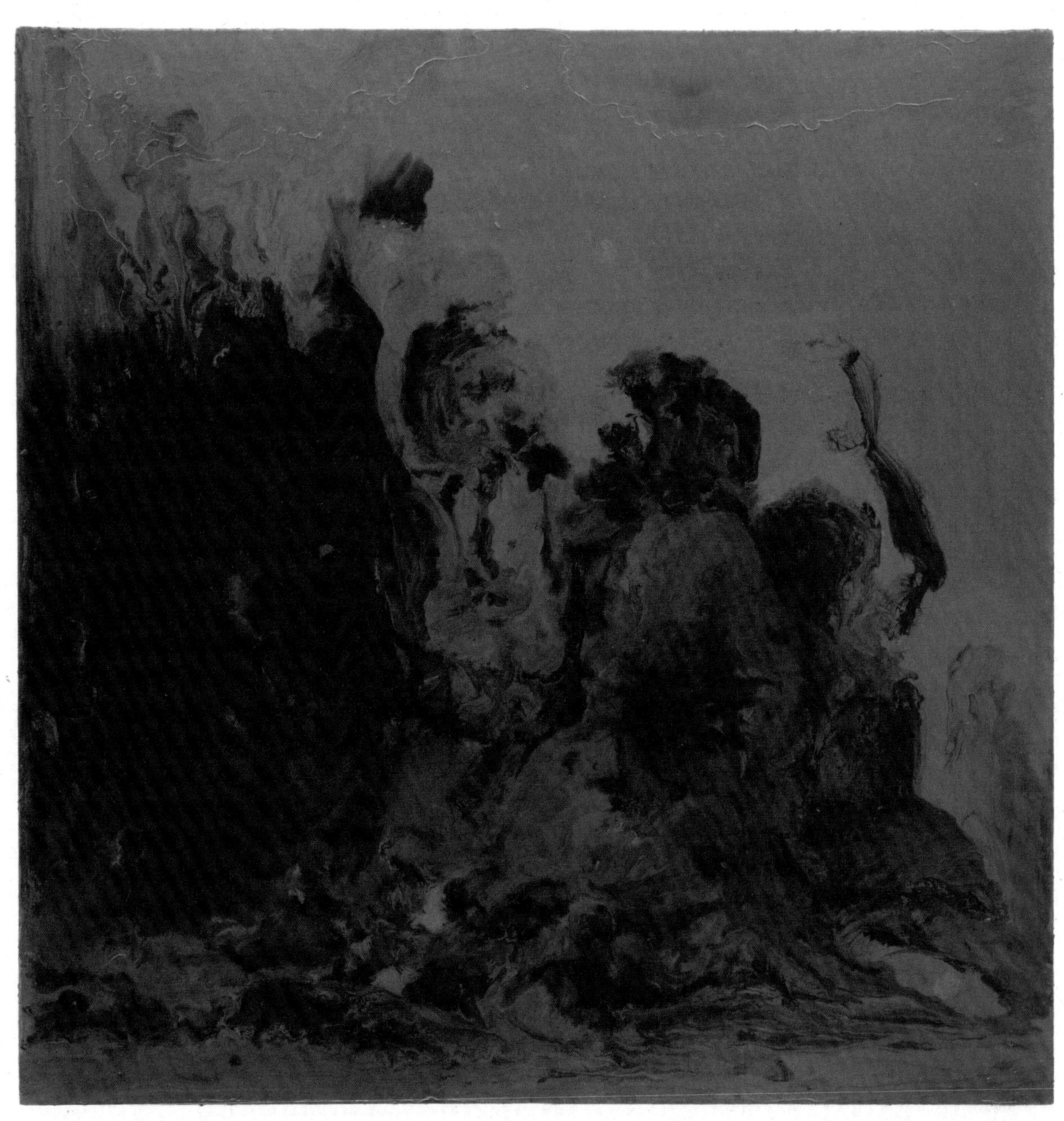

2004
SECOND NATURE
122 x 122 cm

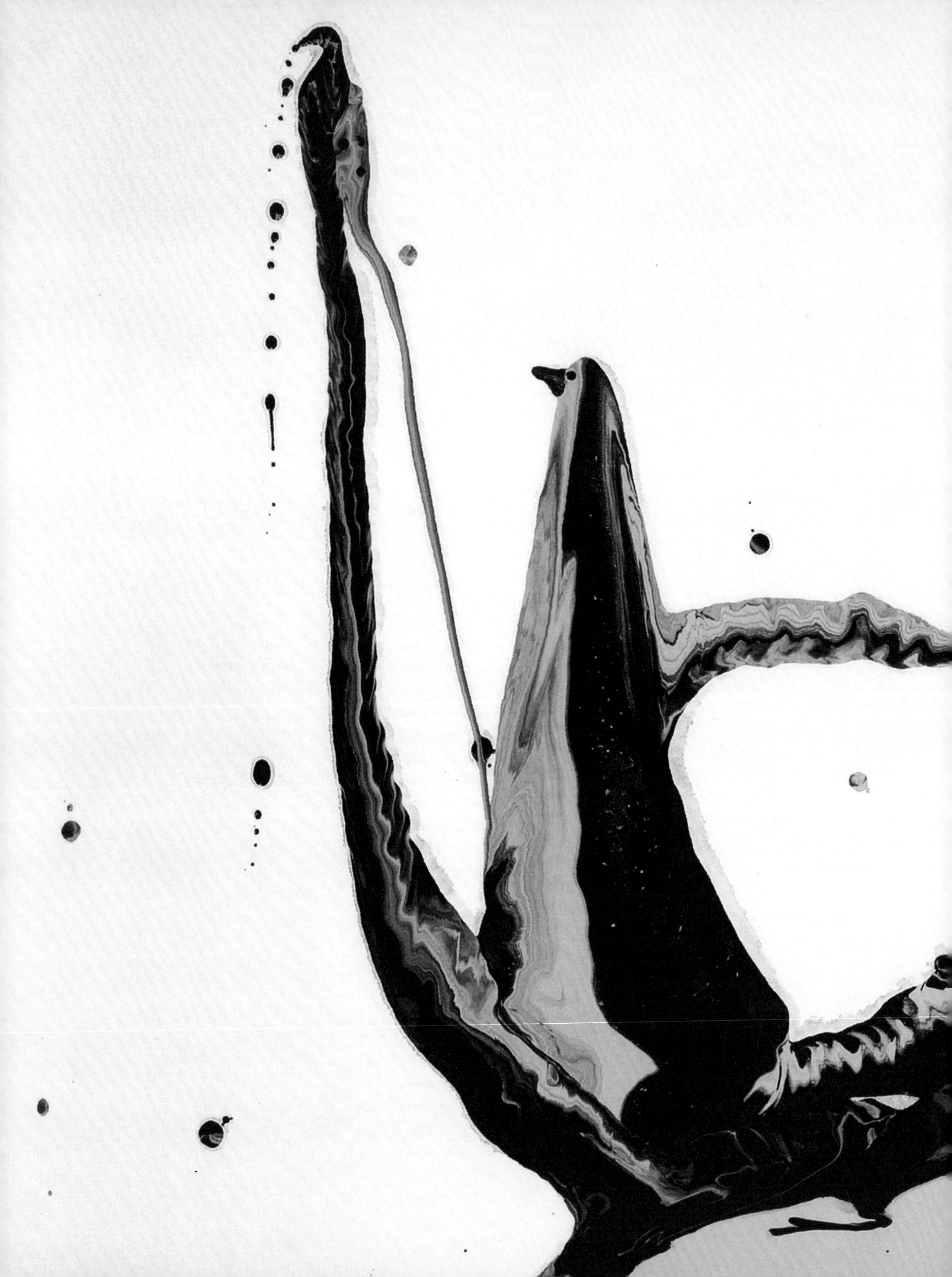

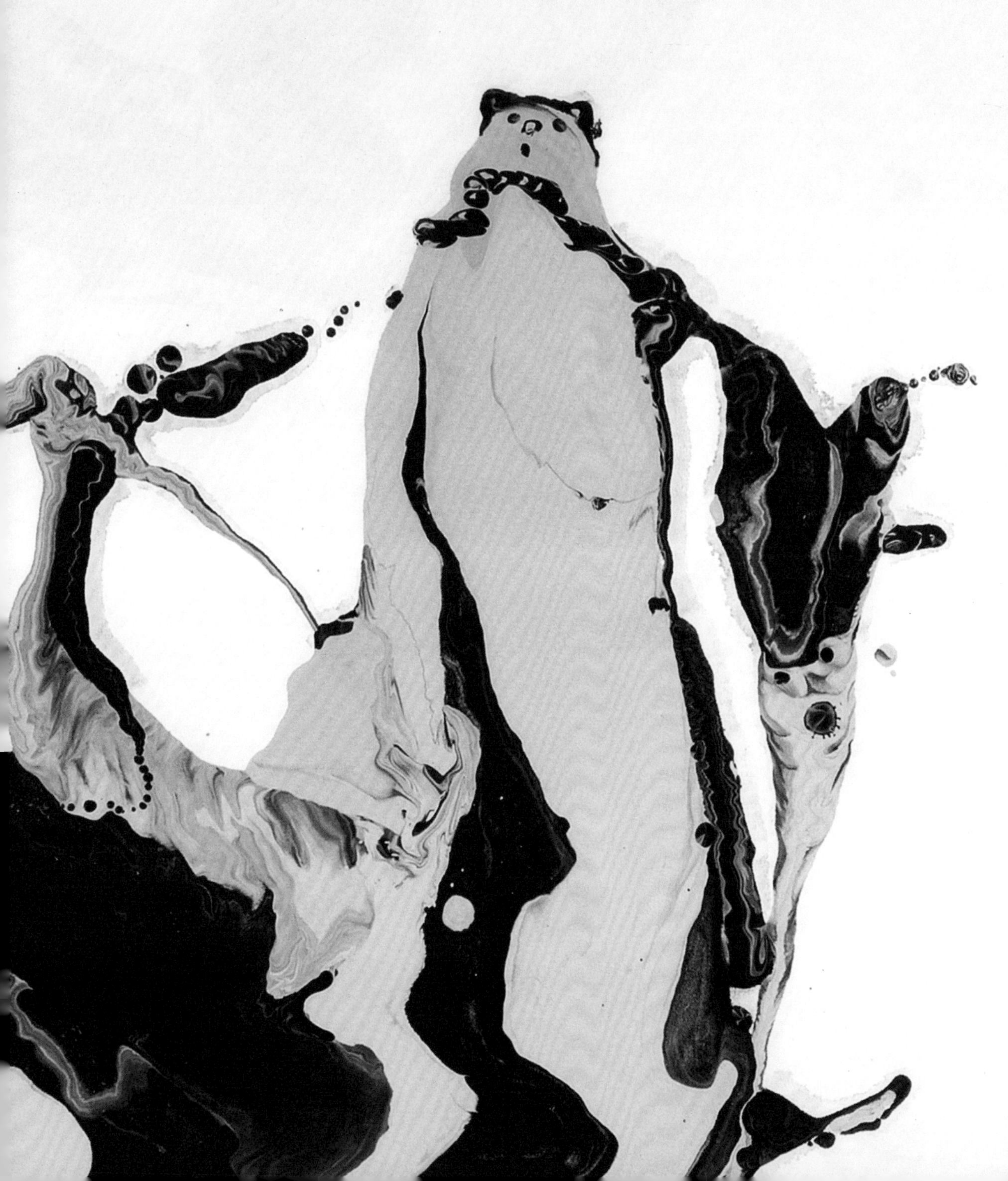

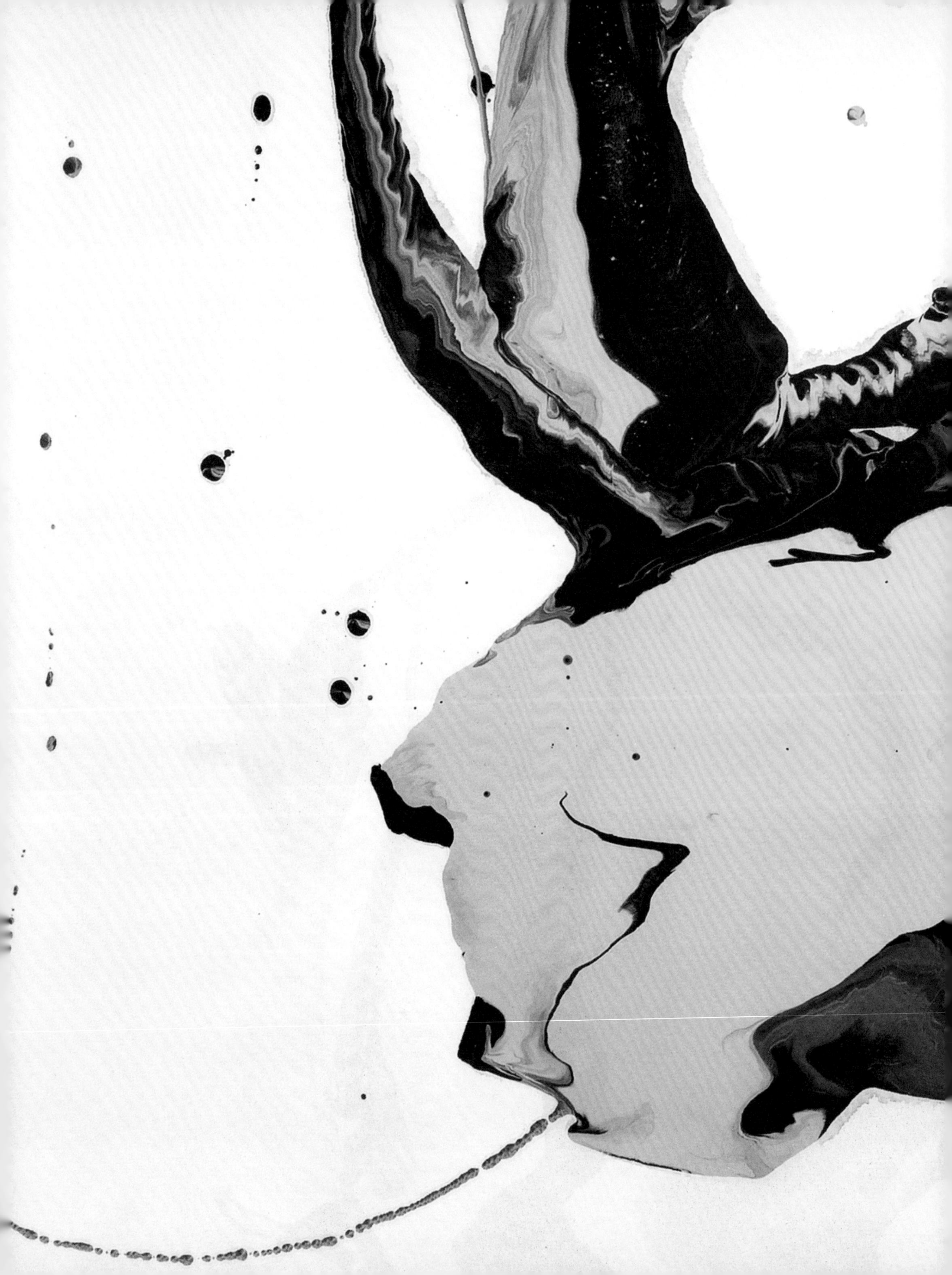

2009
OLD PLANET
130 x 130 cm

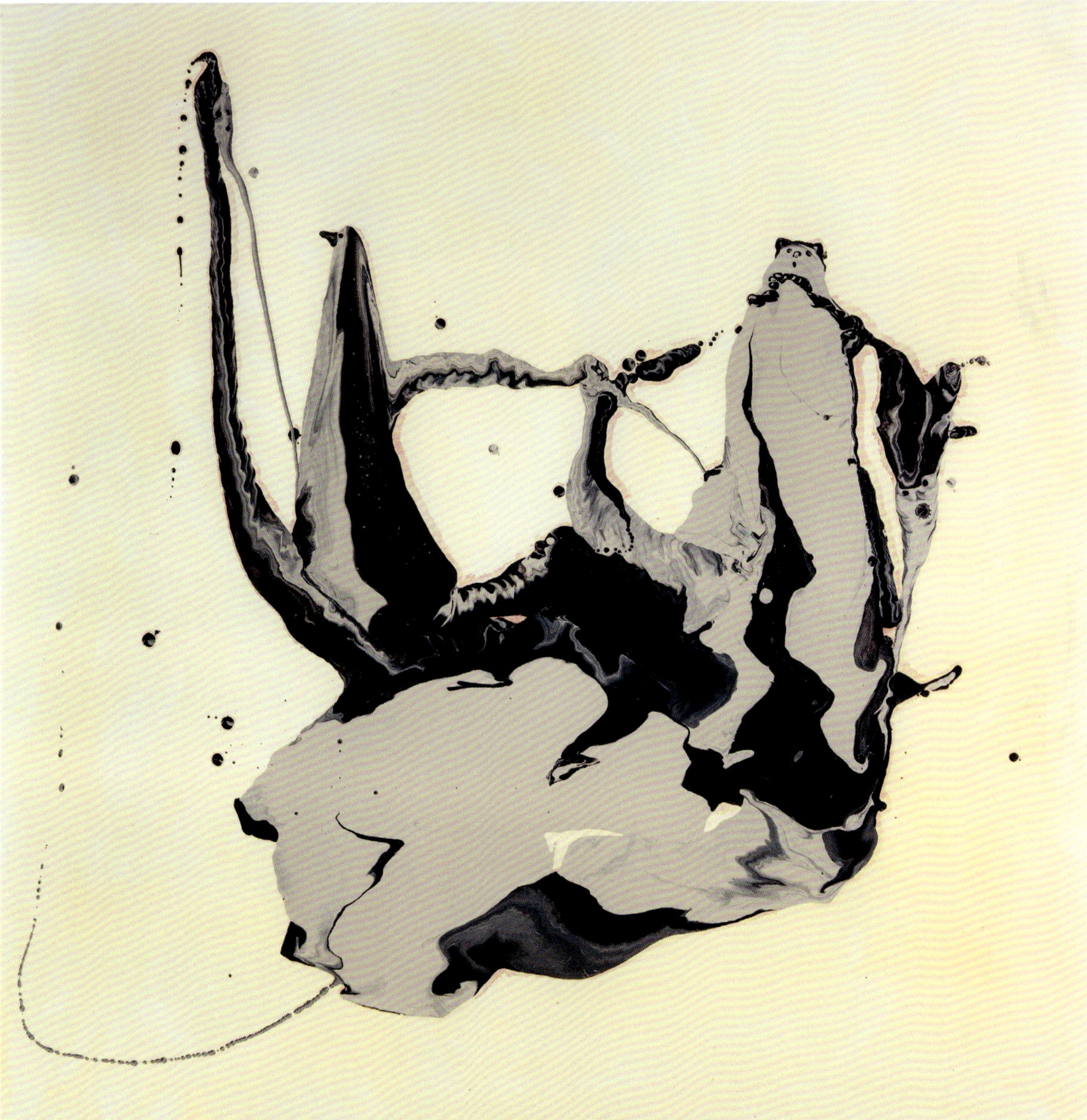

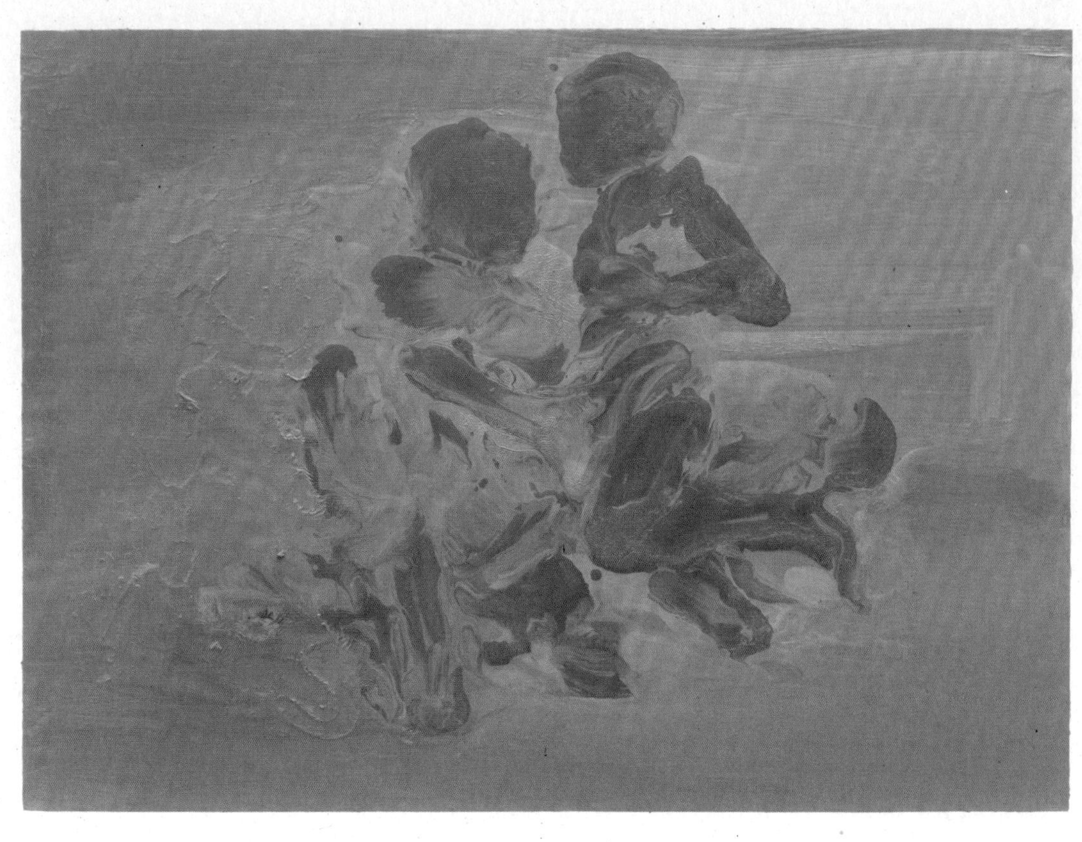

2003
DREAM DREAM
46 x 47.5 cm

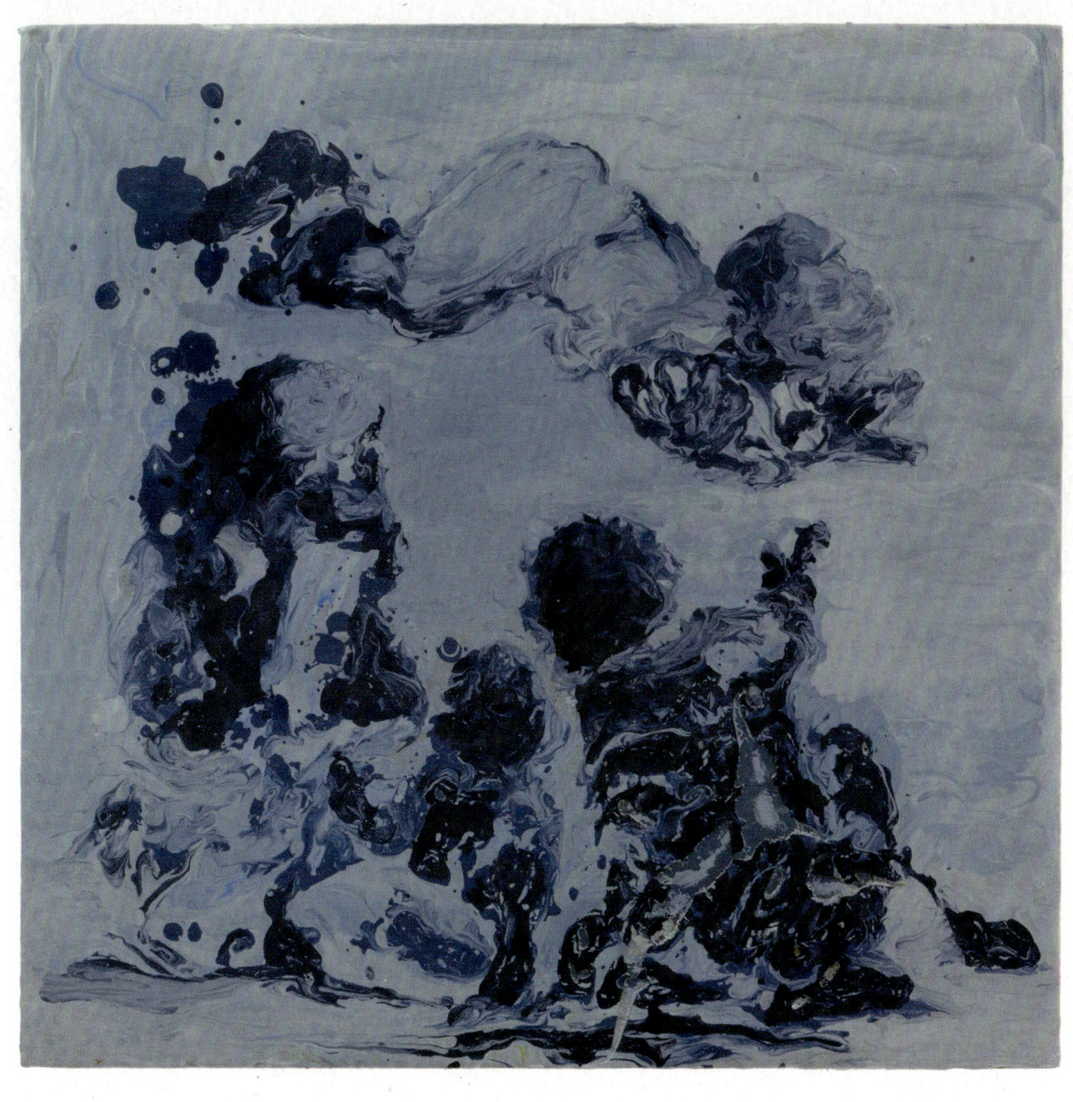

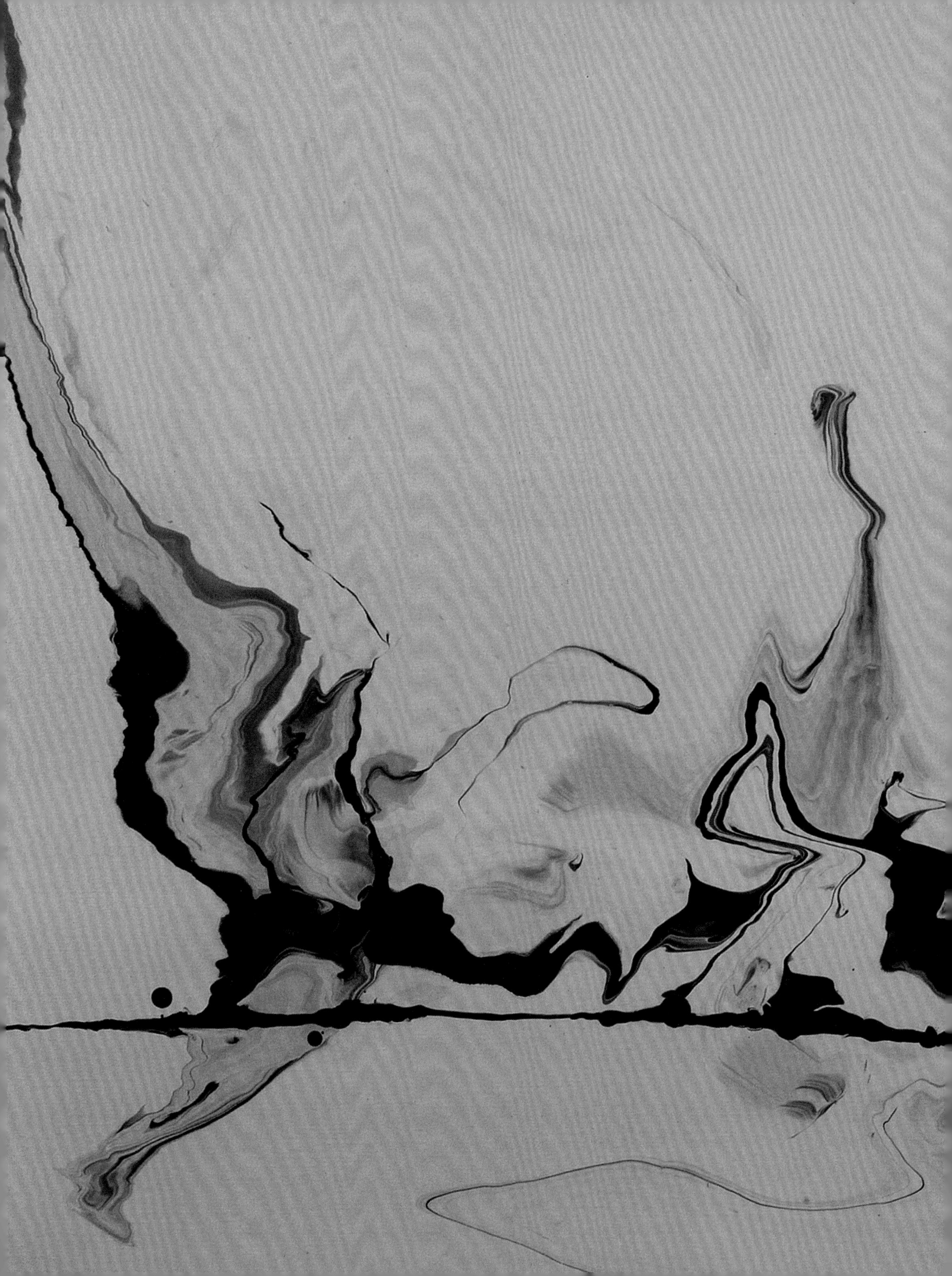

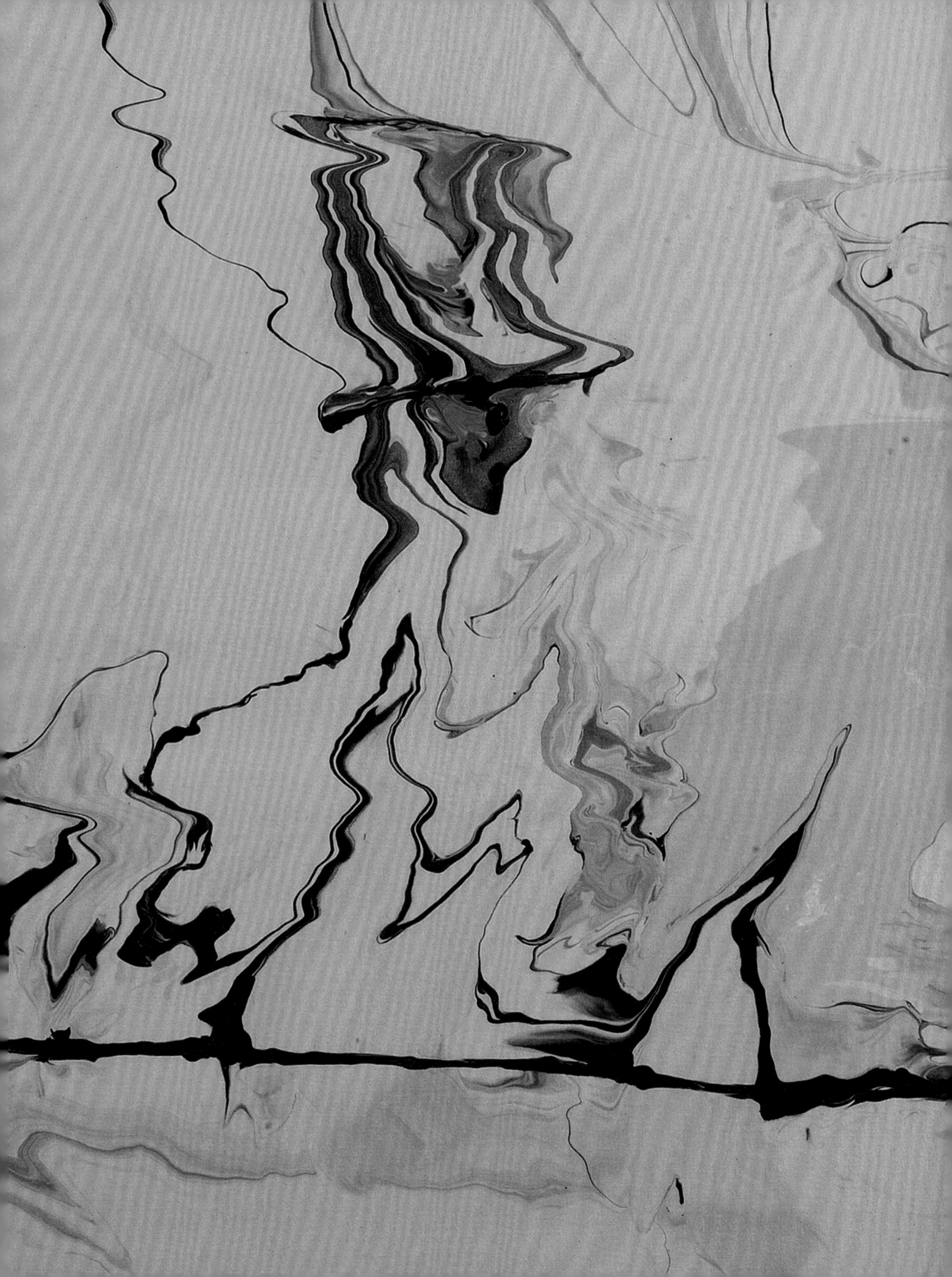

2006
EGO (DEGAS)
151 x 99 cm

pages 34-35
SUBURBIA
(detail, see page 73)

2005
IDEAS OF SOLUTION
152 x 151.5 cm

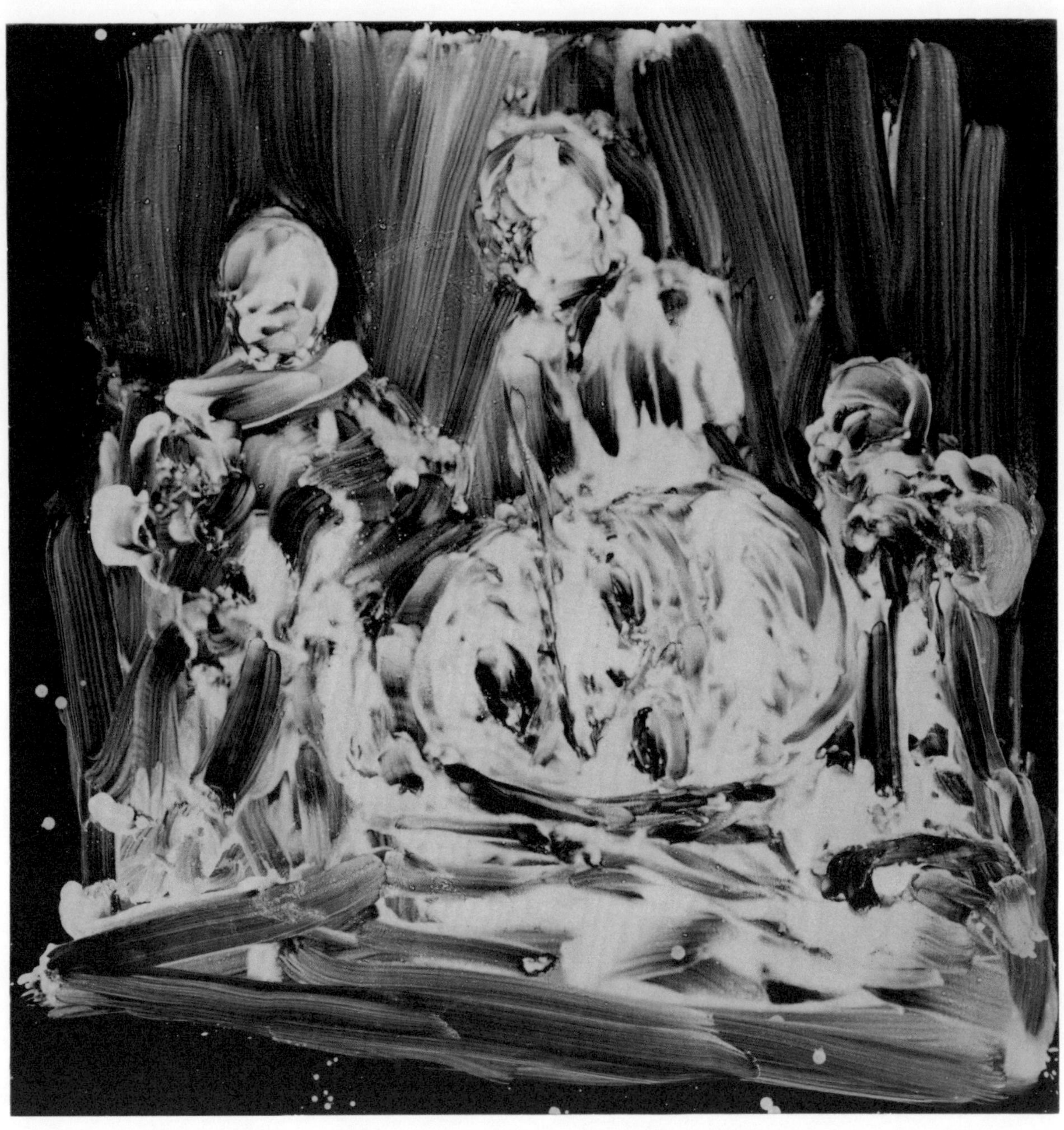

2005
SOUVENIR
122.5 x 121.5 cm

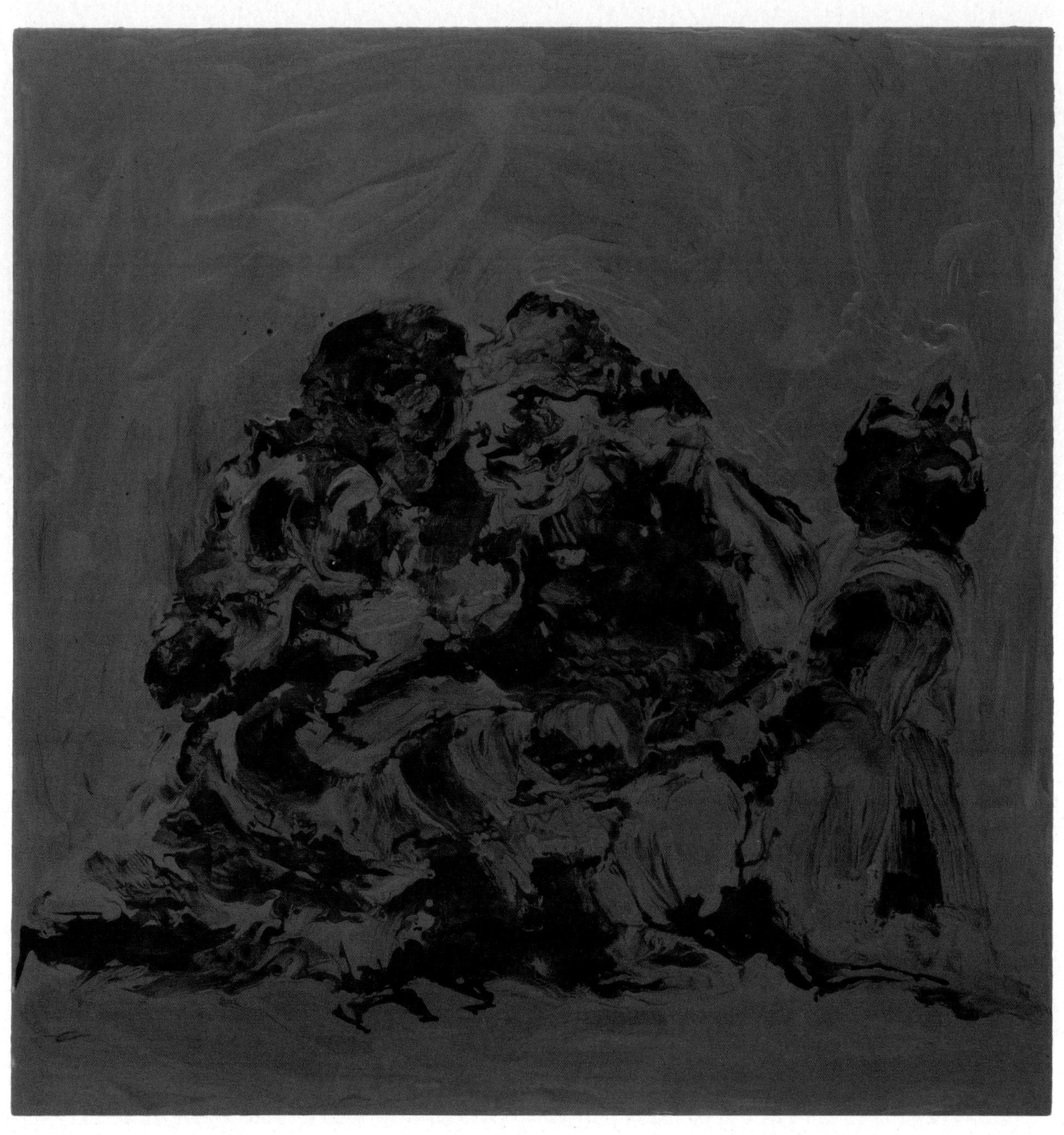

2006
DISPOSSESSION
122 x 122 cm

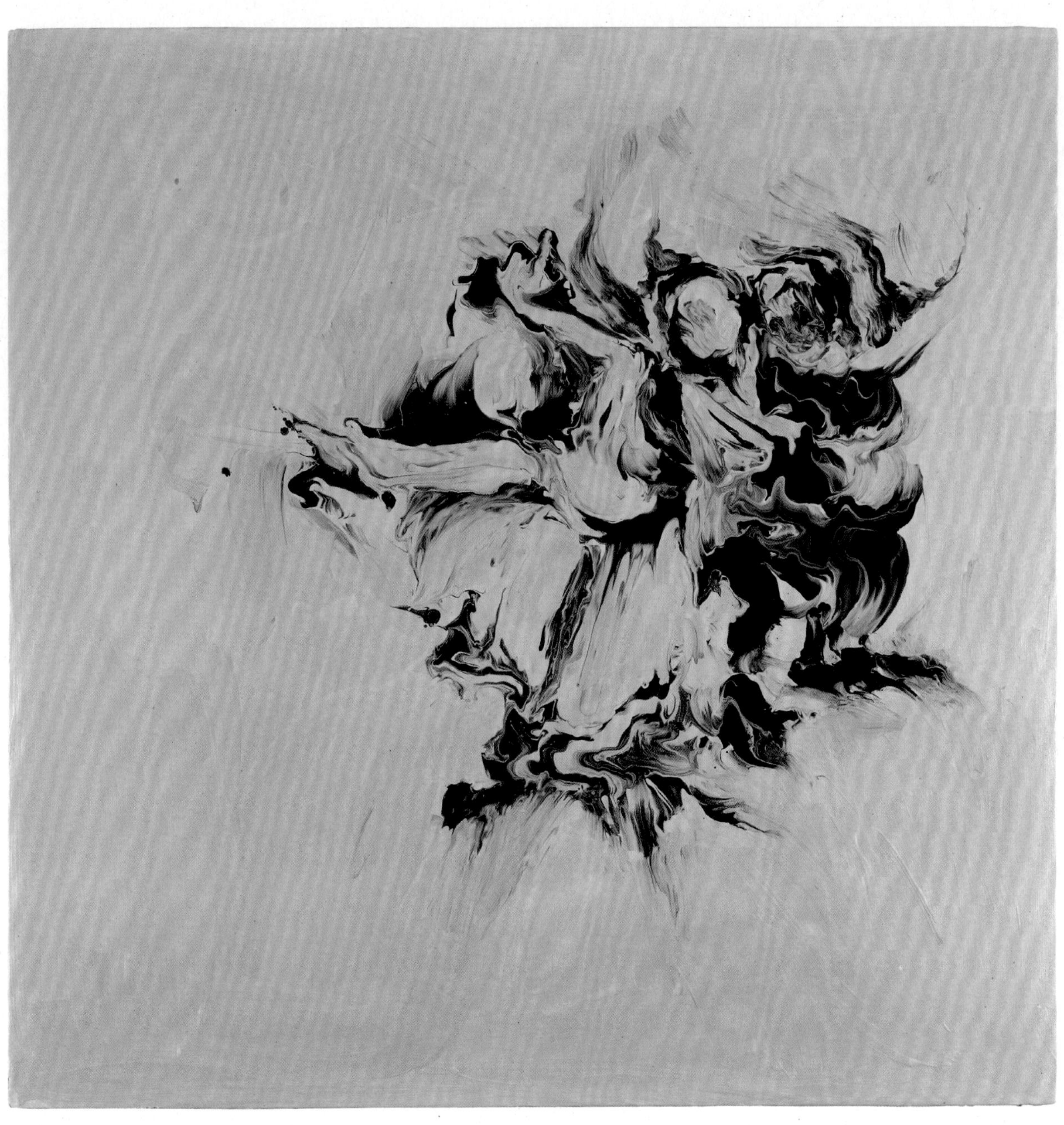

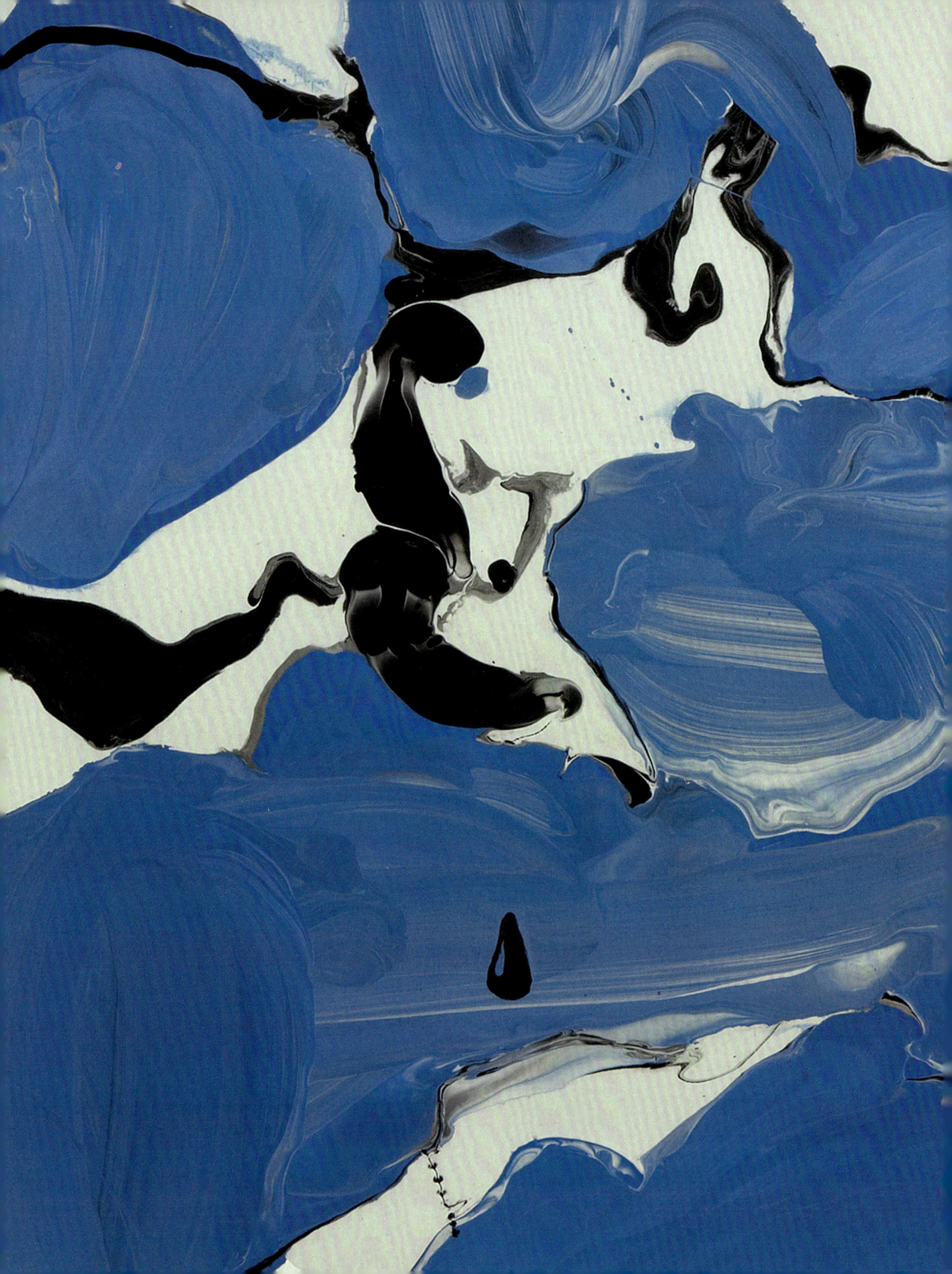

THE PAINTED DROP

LEEN BEDAUX

Existentialist issues in painting lead to a paradox. The atmosphere radiating from the scenes are reminiscent of the carefree life of the nineteenth-century bohemian, while the issues being addressed, on the other hand, are really urgent and perturbing. The nineteenth-century bohemian unreservedly believes in the development of artistic individuality and originality, and is prepared to give up everything for this.

Dresses blown up by the wind, picnic scenes, romantic *tête-à-têtes* set in dreamy landscapes mainly evoke the ideals of the nonchalant bohemian, yet these ideals are simultaneously swamped by a monstrous, sinister drama.

This paradox also has a medium-specific meaning. Rezi van Lankveld approaches the ideals of the bohemian not only in the scenes she depicts, but also in her mastery of materials. By quasi-artlessly deploying the riches of her virtuosity, she demonstratively puts them before other qualities like education, intellectual schooling or functionality. She emphatically refers to artistic individuality and thus to autonomous art. Yet, she is aware that the ideal of the nineteenth-century bohemian clashes with social reality, but it is this very clash that is essential for the understanding of painting today.

A moralist message is hidden in the paintings, which demands contemplation and control in these times of ever accelerating mobility and distribution. Our society is driven by an obsessive urge for change. Constant challenges to believe and belong determine our social climate: always incomplete and never finished, working on continuous identity changes, active in social networks. Conditions in the twenty-first century are changing constantly and so fast that people are no longer able to solidify them into habits and routines. It seems impossible to slow down the enormous speed of change, never mind determining or controlling its direction.

We no longer live in clearly defined communities with comprehensible rules, but in an era in which nothing seems durable and everything is negotiable by everyone at all times. In her paintings, Van Lankveld refers to the tradition of autonomous painting as well as specific (post-)modernist contentious issues. The key question here is whether fine art still has something to contribute, if all definable frames of reference belong to the past and if parameters of space (and time) have also become inadequate. Can a work of art still get a definite shape if everything is always subject to change? Is there still any belief in the power of autonomous art or painting? These and other questions seem to be addressed explicitly.

Liquid Modernity

Current times are characterised by the ephemeral, according to Polish sociologist Zygmunt Bauman, who has been writing about developments within contemporary western society since the 1980s. The arrival of Modernism predicted a future without the whims of nature and its destructive disasters, a future without fear and insecurity. However, modern times have not led to a full control of nature and its capriciousness – even worse, human agency has caused us to be even more exposed to catastrophes on a global level.

Baumann states that uncertainty, worry and fear characterise liquid modernity. Liquid modernity contrasts solid modernity. Solid modernity is rooted in the material world, adheres to enlightened or religious values with a tendency towards social utopias. Liquid modernity, in contrast, is pragmatic: only when it is convenient are historic anchors cast; a real rootedness, however, is missing. While this causes great instability and uncertainty, it also creates a lot of latitude, with lots of options. It is an era in which people have to weigh their options at high speed and have to keep making new decisions. Bauman refers to this as choosing man, or *Homo Eligens*. In their making process, the paintings exhibit an analogy with this liquid modernity. The uncontrollable forces of liquid paint, such as the effects of gravity, the flaring out of thin oil paint, relief and depth of colour highly determine the image of the paintings. This multitude of simultaneous material processes deliver an endless reservoir of images that constantly require decisions about whether to interfere, or not.

Departing from a shapeless liquid mass, the paint is directed by the maker, figurations loom from an indefinable field of matter. A small intervention can make the paint mass change direction, with the result that a completely different figuration floats to the surface.

It is not the chosing man or *Homo Eligens*, but the creating man who is in control. The creative process is halted at some point and the result is, either or not, accepted. In which the last move of the artist is decisive for the image. This last touch is, at the very least, an attempt to restrict and control chaos, that is to say, the catastrophe of uncontrollable forces.

The decision to whether or not accept the result is therefore taken by the artist only. So the final decision that a painting is finished reveals a degree of fundamental belief in makeability.

With this, fine art, or more specific painting with its fixed points of reference, convinces to still to have power of expression.

Liquid tears
A closer look at the painting *Tears* (2009; p.51) could shed more light on this. This painting is part of a series of paintings which evoke the nineteenth-century bohemian to a lesser extent, but really refer more to twentieth-century paintings (whether consciously or subconsciously) such as Edvard Munch's *The Scream*, Willem de Kooning's expressive painterly gestures, or René Daniëls's swans and eyes*. Even though these art historical references are not too obvious, and have perhaps not even been included on purpose, they still are an immanent component of the construction of the image.
* In the painting *The Amused Muse*, 1983.

What is at stake here is that, by means of small references, the paintings carry the entire tradition of painting within them. To a lesser degree, the artistic lifestyle of the bohemian is being idealised here. The air of nineteenth-century artistic life has given way to a more rational construction of image, with a number of subtle references to specific painting icons. As weight is being attached to references to specific subjects from the art of painting, these paintings emphasise the tradition of autonomous art practice more than an exuberant, artistic lifestyle.

This might also explain why the painted drop, or tear, in the painting *Tears*, reminds one of the pearl earring in the painting by Johannes Vermeer, of 1665-1667. The drop has been placed on the canvas here using a similar classic relation like the golden ratio. Just like the pearl, the drop has been painted very precisely with just a few strokes. Similar highlights point to the sparkling solid surface, in the case of the pearl, and to a transparent liquid matter, in the case of the drop. So both solid and liquid forms are brought remarkably close together here.

Thus, whether it was done consciously or subconsciously, the painting is rooted in art history. Or, in more general terms, a lot of import is attached to the retention of roots. These are no non-committal references, no postmodern Spielerei that would undermine the authenticity of other painters, but a deeply rooted belief in the art of painting. So this painting does not at all exhibit a postmodern alienation, but rather an inextricable connection to the tradition of painting. In that sense, the work is open to modern as well as postmodern interpretations.

The drop unfolds a dichotomy of being and representing it, which is expressed in the liquidity of the paint and the painted shape of the drop. The cliché-like shape of the drop mainly renders it into a course symbol without emotional charge. It is a pictogram that represents the wet-on-wet painting technique and the analogy with liquid modernity. Thus, the painted drop contrasts sharply with the rest of the painting, which is permeated by a painterly stratification that presents itself as an immediate and direct aesthetic experience.

The carefully placed details seduce the viewer to try and fathom the story behind the scene. The sensuality of matter and material control seamlessly merge into the sensuality of the figuration. There is the thrill of finding or not finding figurations that are purposely kept in an instable balance. It almost seems as if the figurations which sometimes loom up, and at other times don't, mock het pathos of painting and heavily charged analogies; but at the same time mockery is out of the question, since the painterly art is taken very seriously.

The title heavily refers to the emotional side of the painting. This not only stresses a dramatic mood, but also forces the viewer into a certain way of reading the painting. The drop cannot be understood as anything but a tear. From this tear a cartoonlike human figure looms up among the pools of paint and the brush strokes. A prosaic story emerges and pushes aside every experience of a purely painterly account in the matter. What dominates is the image of an introvert human being catching his own tears in an open hand holding an elegant necklace.

Having once perceived the tear and its matching figuration, it cannot be revoked. As a result, the painterly expression, the virtuoso handling of matter can no longer be experienced as unperturbed, direct aesthetic imagery. The tear thereby also seems to refer to the sorrow of the inadequacy of painting. The hand catching the single tear can be interpreted as an ultimate attempt not to have to lose the art of painting.

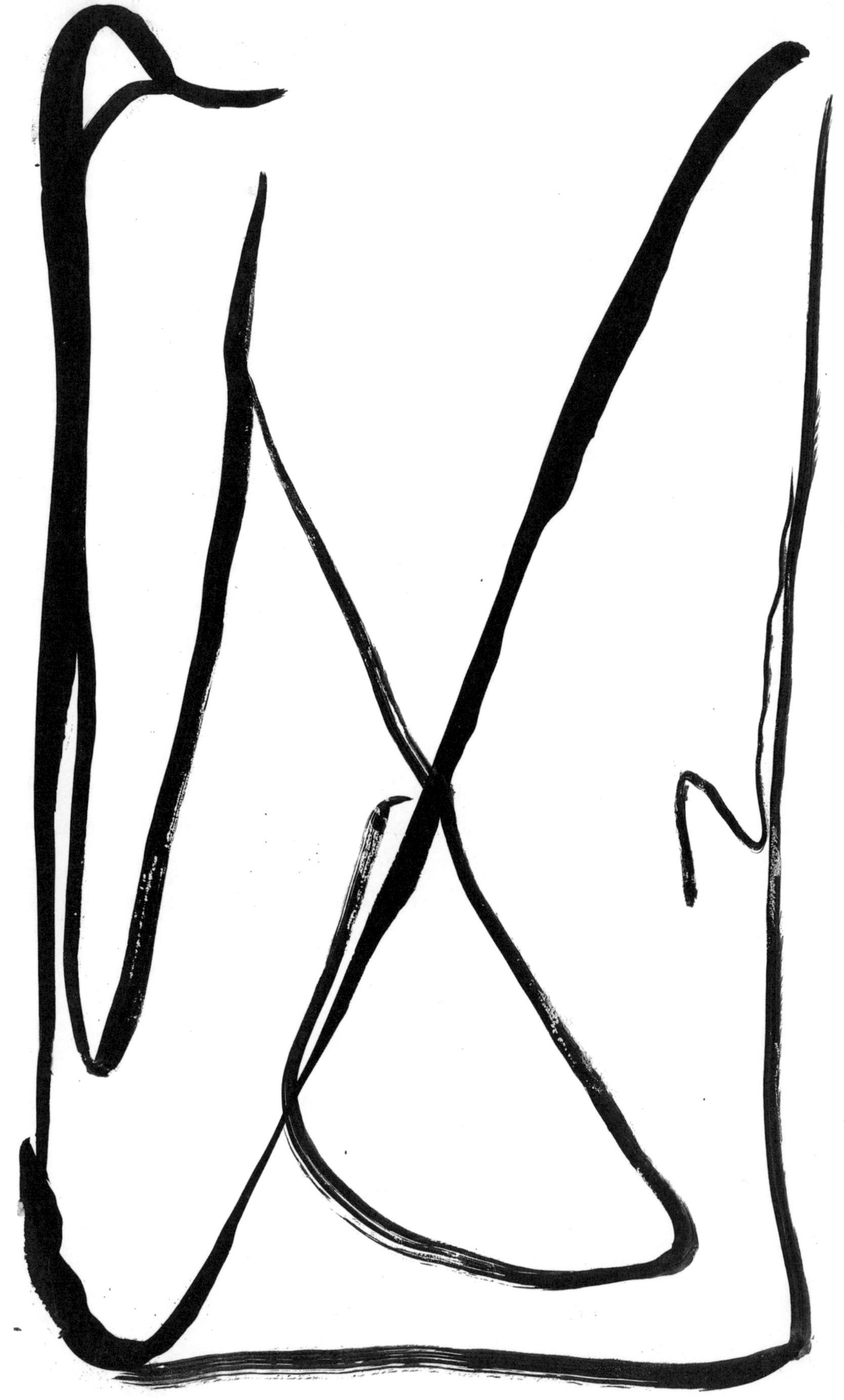

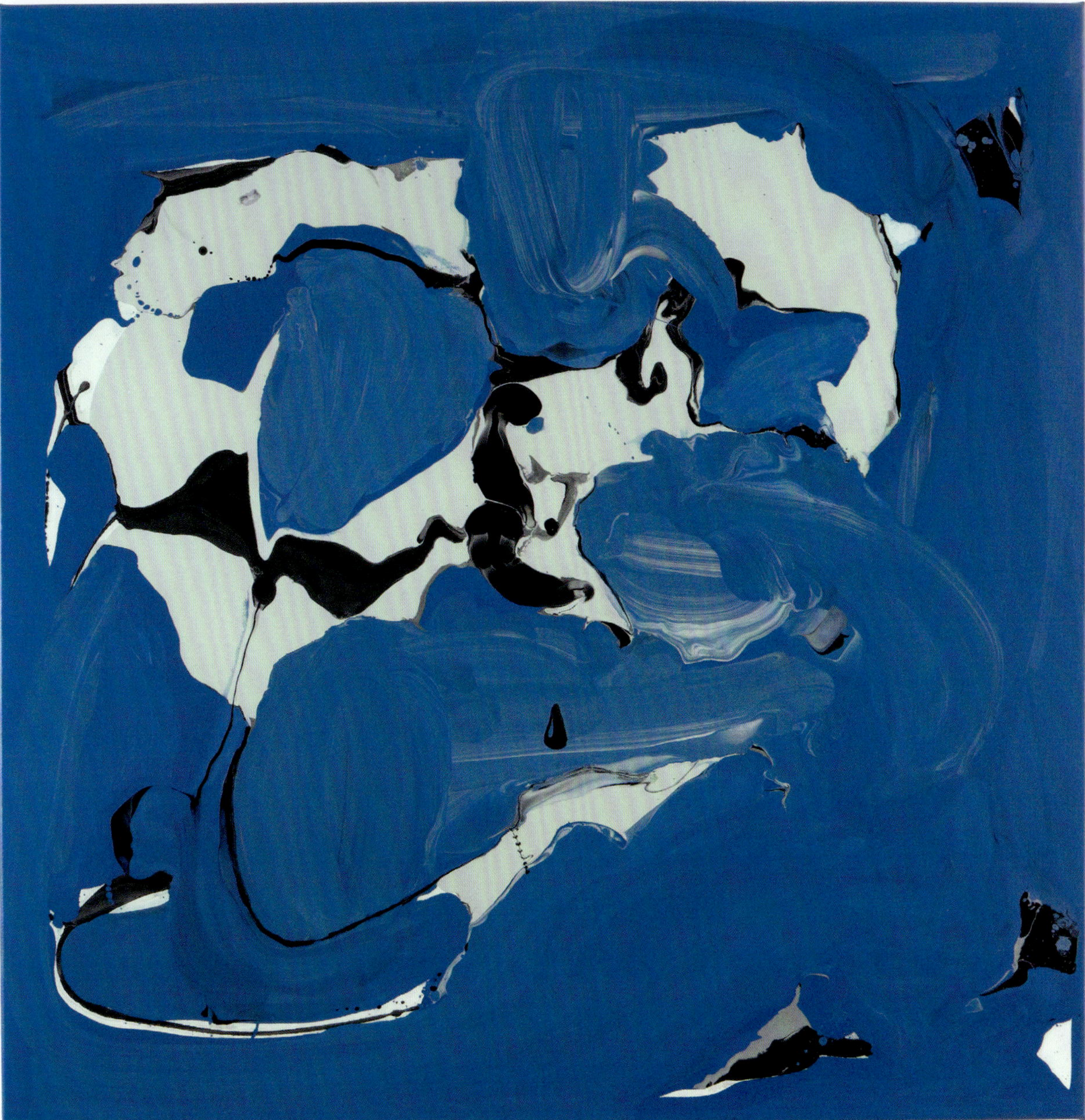

2009
TEARS
120 x 120 cm

2007
LISTEN
63 x 60 cm

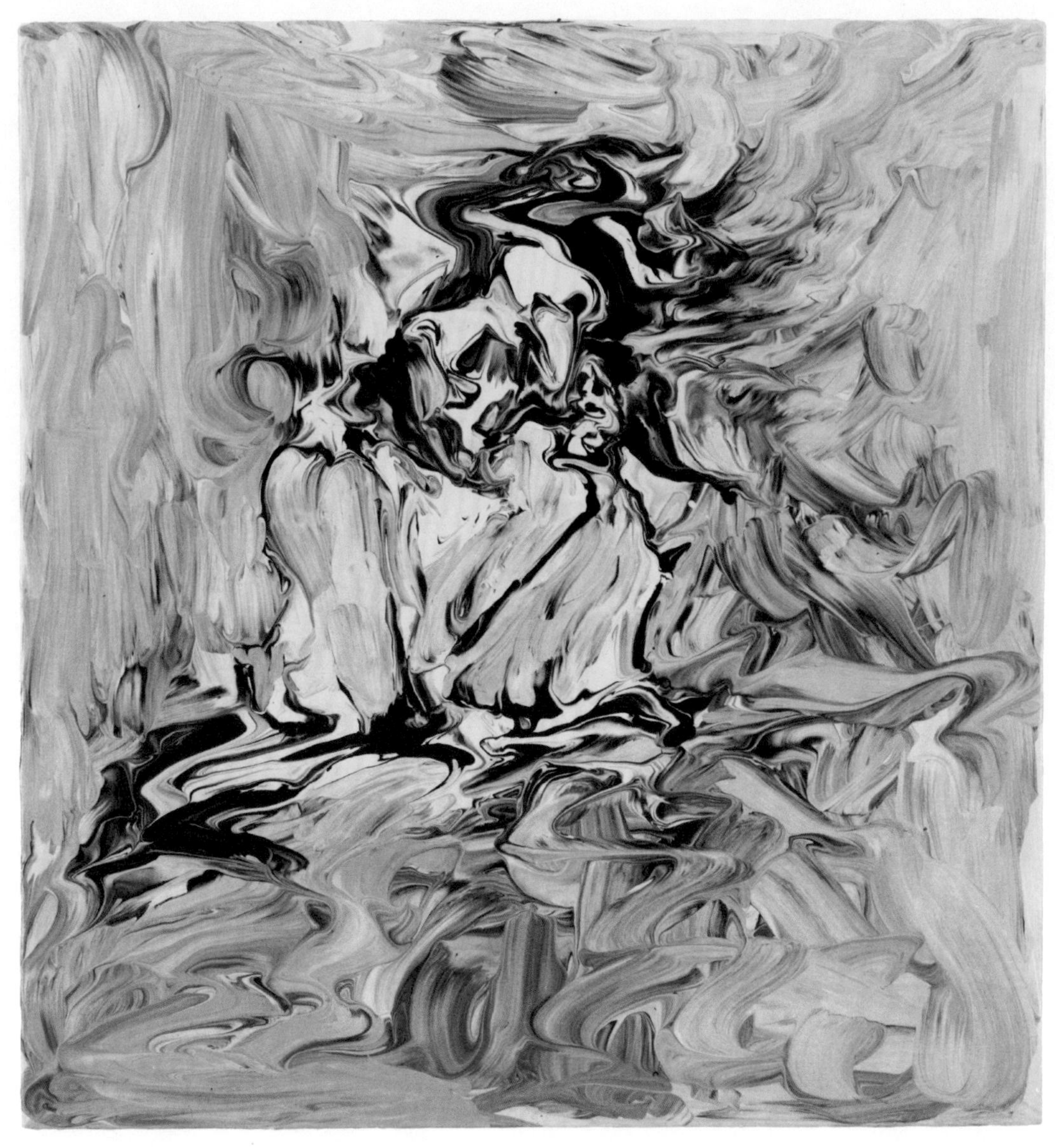

2006
A MON SEUL DÉSIR
122 x 122 cm

76311
~~RE~~ 984-2

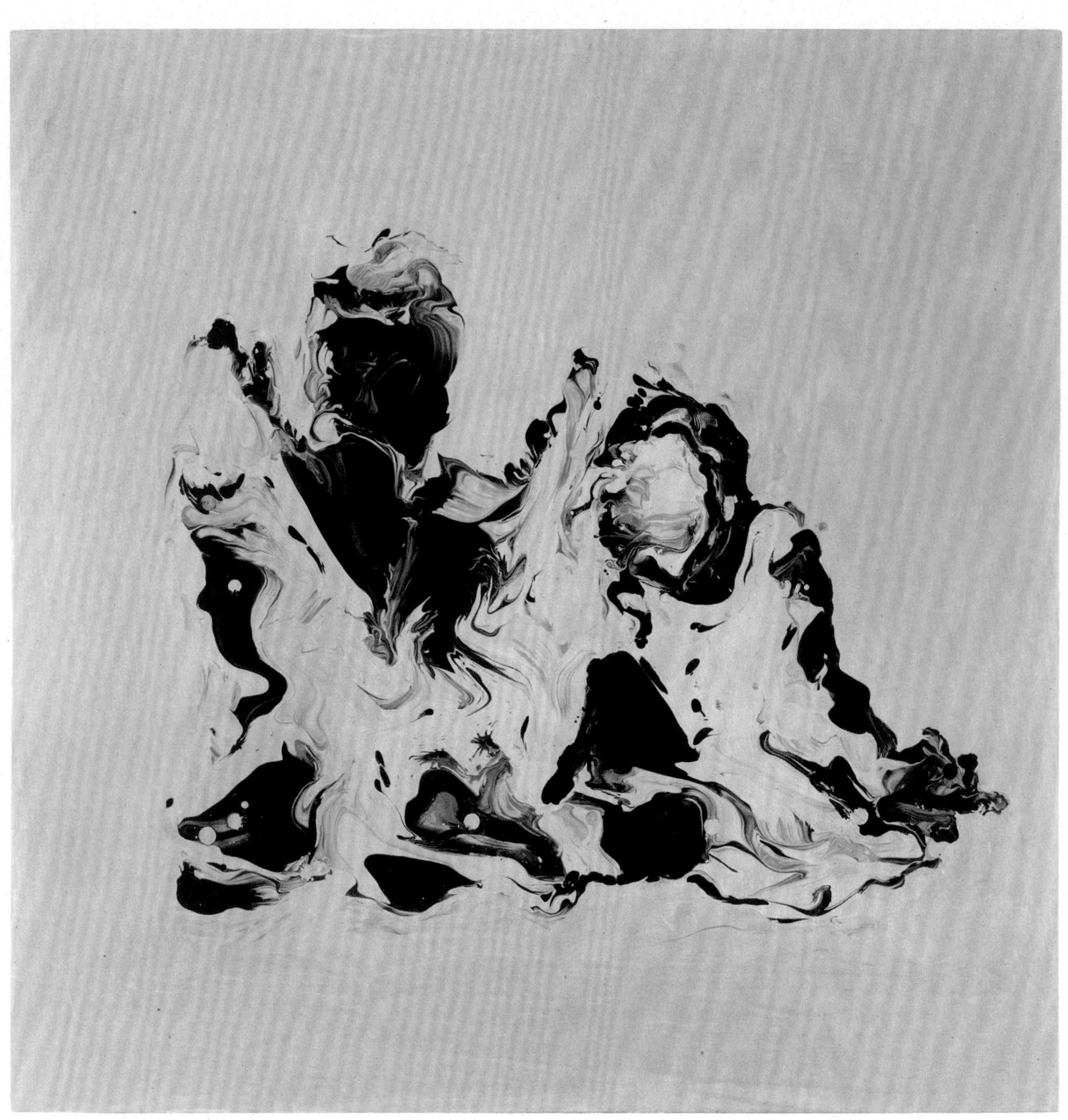

2006
LITTLE BLUE RAPE
32 x 35 cm

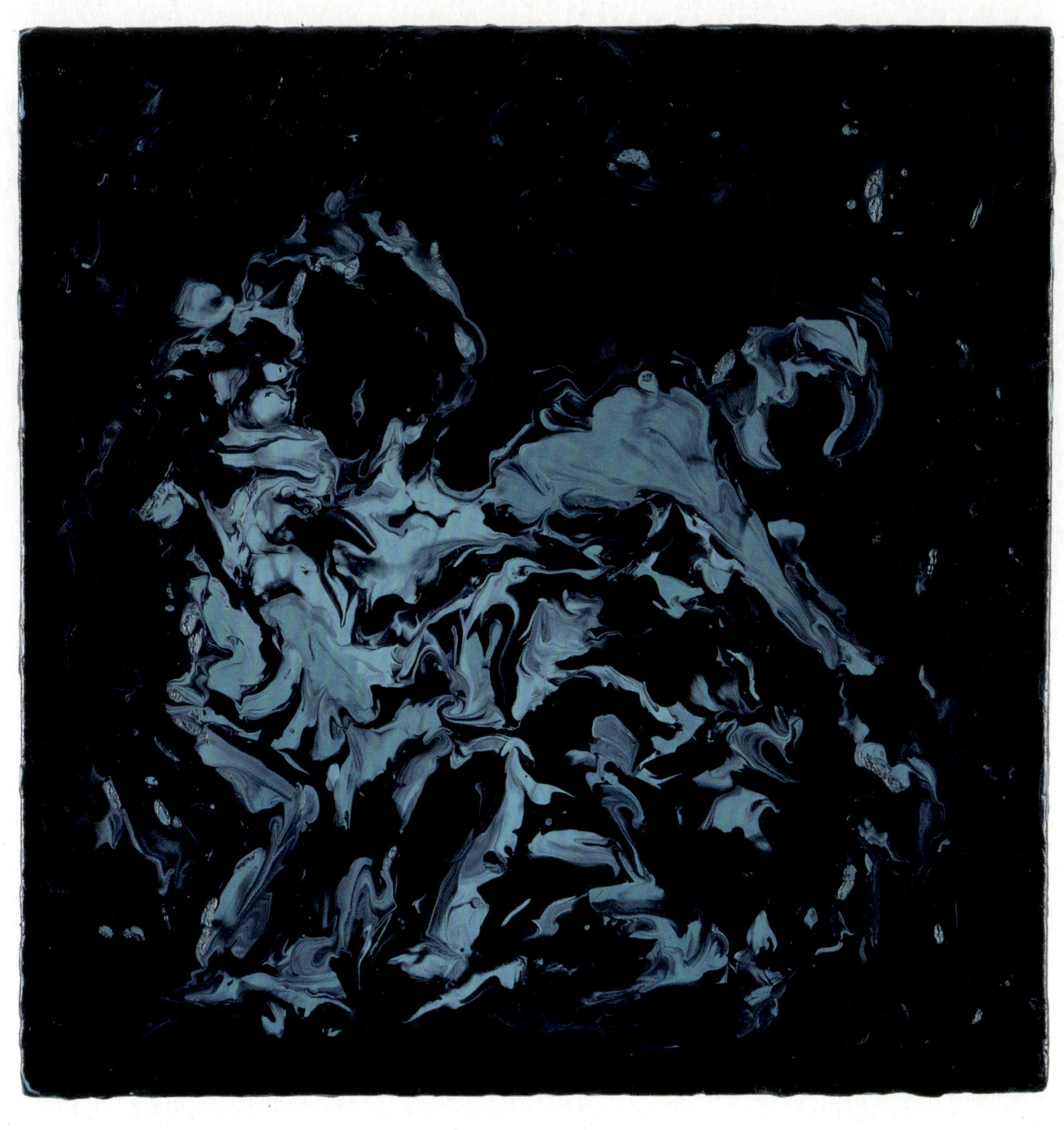

2007

THERE WAS A YOUNG LADY
FROM HELL WHO JUMPED
AT THE SOUND OF A BELL
BECAUSE SHE WAS BAD-BAD-BAD

135 x 121.5 cm

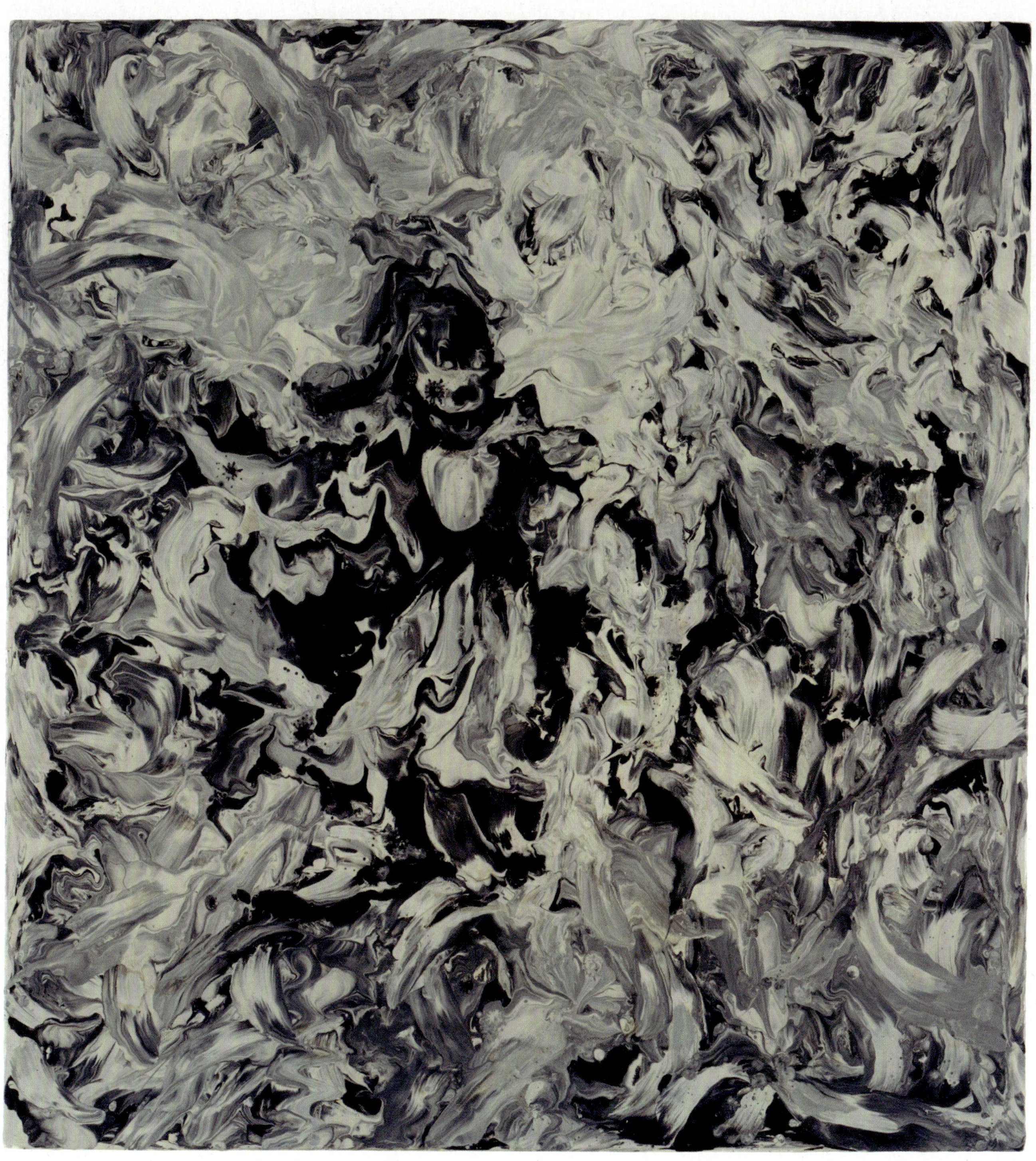

2007
ROCK
120 x 120 cm

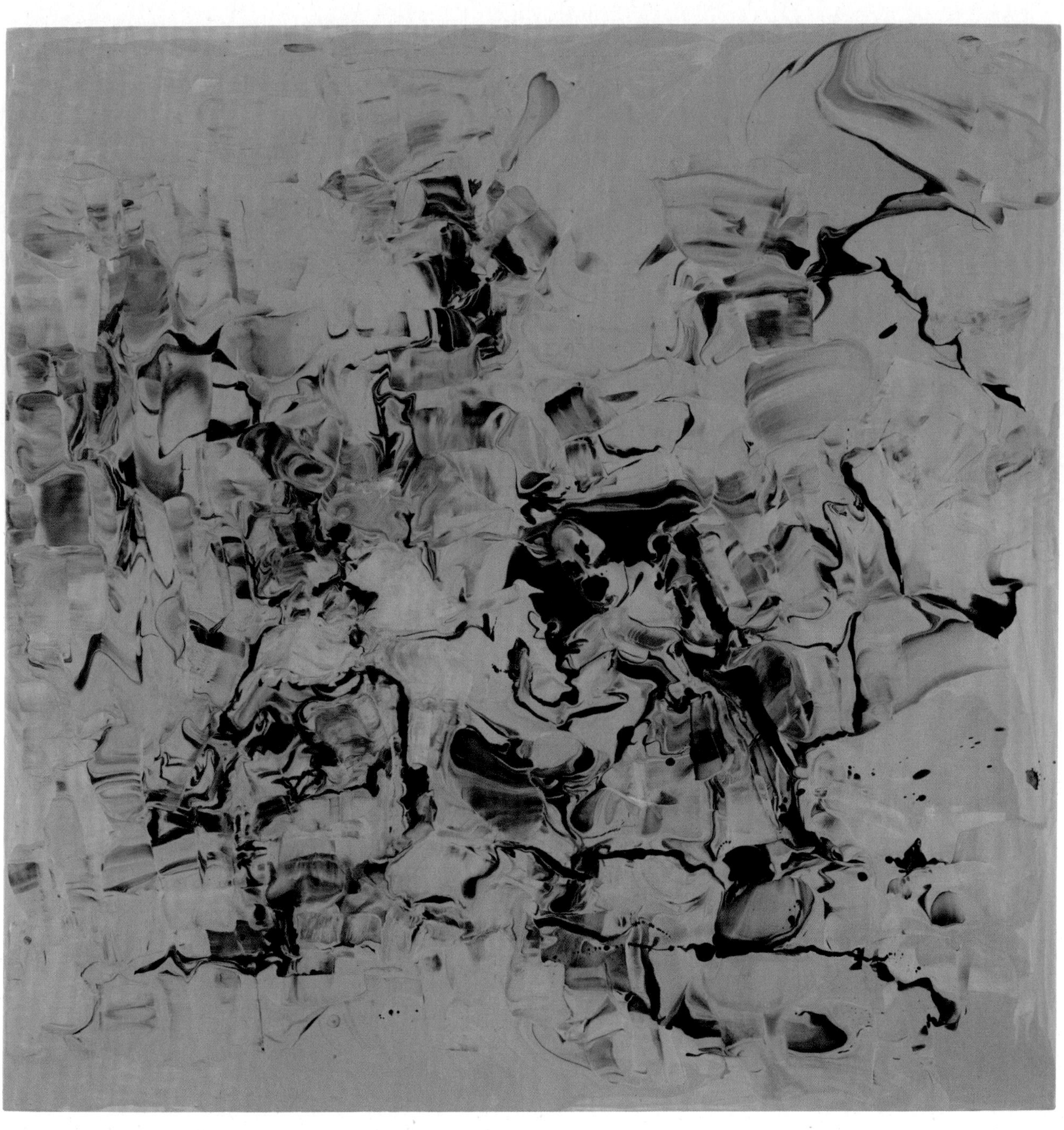

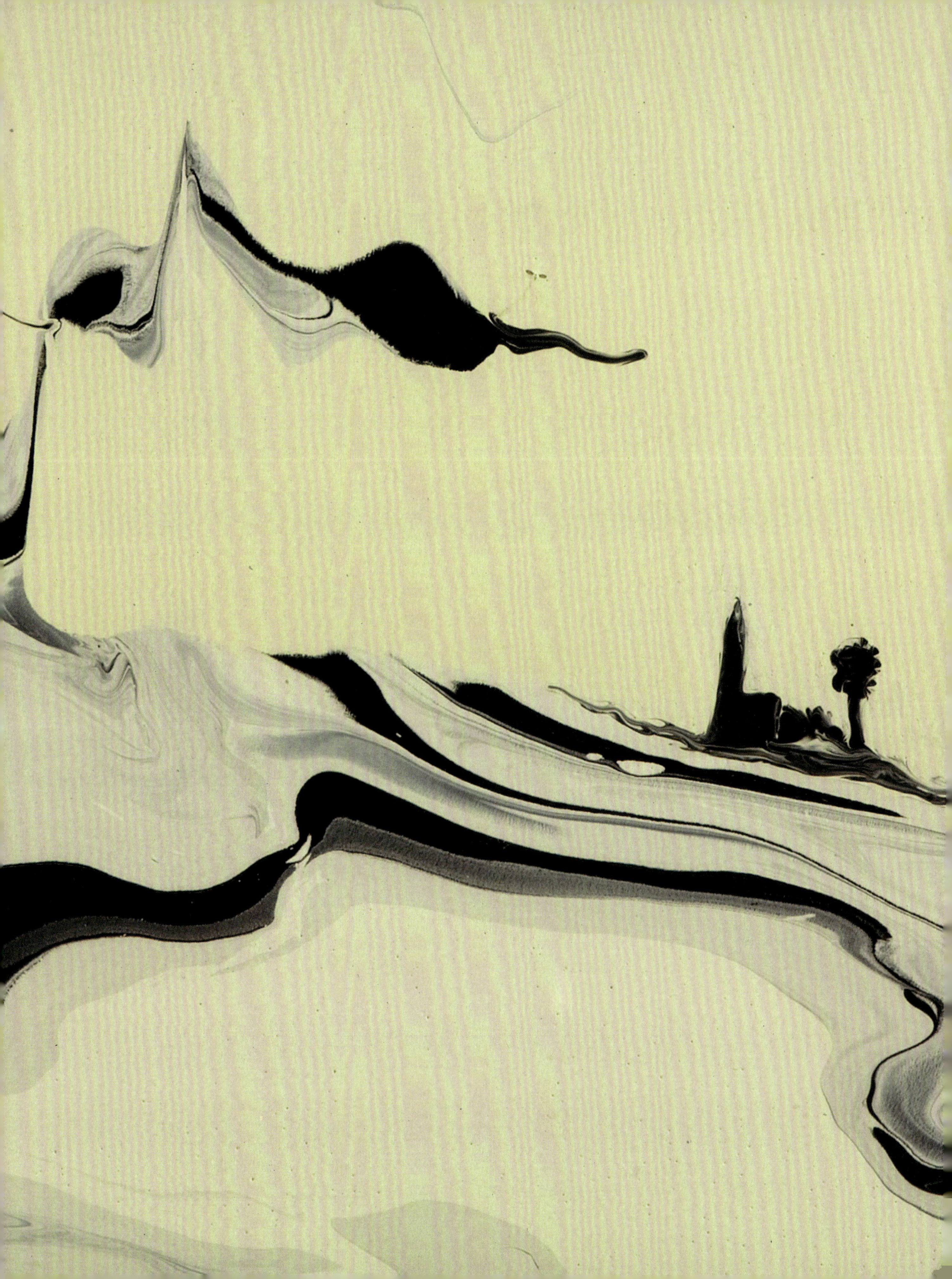

ONE SHOT

JEREMIAH DAY

What is at stake in the minor revelation, the modest image and human-scale drama?

—

An earlier catalogue of Rezi van Lankveld has been inscribed to me with the words *'it could all be worse!'*

Death of painting. You hear stories. CalArts in the eighties, painters chased out of group critiques: "and take your wallpaper with you!" But I've been to Eli Broad's temple, a tower building on the beach to house his collection, and it is beautifully decorated with works by Hans Haacke that critique Shell Oil, *et al.*

In other words, when it seems like the most "critical" artworks can serve quite nicely as *decoration*, then such instrumentalisation must be measured in degrees, fractions even.

So those paintings – they hang on the wall, look nice, are they only décor? (Any defense undertaken in words would be a losing effort – he 'doth protest too much' – so judge for yourself, oneself.)

The choreographer replied "I don't believe in improvisation. It doesn't exist. Really there is only real-time composition." Claims to spontaneity, immediacy and intuition are over-stated, he was suggesting, instead there is the accumulative process of decisions and execution, judgment, decisions and execution.

For the engaged public of "real-time composition," watching and hearing Pharaoh Sanders or some other jazz practitioner for example, we are present for the process, along for the ride. We too can judge and decide, but we have to see where the musician wants to go, to execute, and we have the thrill of surprise, confirmation, occasional disappointment. Still disinterested in our own needs, problems, but not a detached spectator. During the horn solo, the piano player repeats his riff over and over again, providing a structure for the soloist to work against, an act of support. Our presence in the room similarly functions as support, and perhaps even, at some moment, we can feel as if perhaps we add something through our witnessing, our active engagement and attention.

In the period when improvisational music was practiced and discussed most seriously, the production, distribution and sales of records took on a different aspect. The records were literally just that, artifacts of an arc or phrase of real-time composition, documented clearly and the offered up through distribution to the those were "into it." *Ascension* by John Coltrane, or even earlier *Free Jazz: A Collective Improvisation* by Ornette Coleman, are structured primarily by their end points – cut in, cut out – a 40 minute episode captured for posterity, with the duration decided by the length of the standard long-play vinyl album. Even more than the decisions made within the session – with players judging when to step into the foreground of attention, when to pull back and make space for another, or even holding back altogether, the explicit absence that makes forming negative space into a conscious and concrete decision – and even more than the quality of the playing (and one cannot forget the relentless technical honing that these musicians demand of themselves), the aesthetic statement of such works is primarily the relationship between process and product, the insistence on the primacy of the "live" moment, with the finished vinyl, cd, or now mp3 standing as a relic.

In this way it is not without interest to note that this chapter of jazz was effectively concluded with Miles Davis' *Bitches Brew*, when Davies's broke with this aesthetic principle and decided to use studio techniques — "post-production" — as not only a tool of documentation but one of active composition and craft.

The parallels between real-time composition in jazz and in painting have been undertheorized and underappreciated, most likely because of the difference in social milieu, although some of John Coltrane's statements about his ultimately metaphysical concerns sound quite a chord with those of Mark Rothko or Barnett Newman, and both shared a conception in which aesthetic practice maintained the possibility of broader effect, if not political than at least humanist. But while posterity and even the critics of the time did not pursue this shared aesthetic ethos, the practitioners themselves were quite aware of it, as is made most explicit with Ornette Coleman's use of Jackson Pollock's *White Light* for the cover of Coleman's *Free Jazz*. (And interestingly, to return to the question of the dismissal of painting as decorative, many great essays have been written exploring the use of Pollock's work as a backdrop for *Vogue Magazine* in 1951, but little attention has been made to Coleman's appropriation of Pollock and what this intersection might reveal.)

One echo or legacy of this relationship between real-time composition and painting is the question occasionally heard in group critiques of paintings in art schools: "what do you think the last move was?" In other words, what was the decision that made the painting "done"? Because this decision is of a different nature than the others, this is the decision which cuts the process, not interrupting it, but ending it and thus defining it's essential wholeness. In the hierarchy of decisions, even more than in jazz, when to finish a painting is the most important as from that point forward working gives way to "a work," and a movement through time crystallizes to a statement in space. One "climbs a mountain because it is there," one makes art "because it is not," as Carl Andre said, and this mountain which will stand in posterity will always ring through with the echo of this final decision — how to finish. Like the forty minute limit which defines the albums mentioned above, the decisive move which animates and structures the work of Rezi van Lankveld is the achievement of an image, after which a painting is decided to be done, and the long route of thinking through this musical tradition is hopefully a helpful way of preparing for a consideration of her practice. Working wet-on-wet, or in other words working in and through single continuous process of engagement with the material her finished works are similarly episodes of play and struggle, artifacts of compositional decisions, and like the decision what not to play, the rigor and fostering of attention, the preparing the ground and gathering of focus to attend to the process - as if the atmosphere of judgment and timing itself could be conveyed — all this ineffable substance becomes the main communicative content of the work. What is at stake in this re-shuffling of the traditional role of process dissolving into product, both in general and in these works of Van Lankveld? Donald Judd was so captivated by the way an artwork could exist as a relic of a decision, that after writing about what came to be known as *"one shot"* painting (the term most closely associated with Helen Frankenthaler, Kenneth Noland, and others), Judd developed a theory that such works broke from the European "part/whole, relational" composition, and the entire rationalistic philosophy it accompanied. Taking this up into his own artworks, which were products of a single idea articulated through a non-artistic process of fabrication, "conceive > execute," Judd grandly asserted that his work contained a whole new statement, a more accurate "open" philosophical model of non-deterministic encounter.

Such ambitious statements could not be further from the role of the artist posited by Van Lankveld. Even the tendency towards heroism in the painterly gesture is counter-acted by the insistence on whimsy and a light touch. Furthermore, contrary to the entire community of peers from which she emerged, Van Lankveld's practice is the opposite of the world traveler, or appropriation of larger and larger methods of production. Van Lankveld rarely travels and is reluctant to take on a studio assistant for even drudgerous tasks. Though the work does not display technical virtuosity, there is a clear commitment to a practice. Like John Coltrane coming home from a gig and then working another hour or two more on his horn at home, only not blowing any sound so as to not wake the children, the rigor conveyed by her body

of work is that of a commitment to attending to one's own way. But rather than be distracted by any false modesty, what is at stake in this broader aesthetic ethos which this practice clearly shares, is a problemization of the status of means and ends, action and fabrication. My use of these terms is informed by the work of Hannah Arendt, wherein the distinction between work and action was that work maintains a means-ends relationship, and all is subjugated to the final product. Action on the other hand is the initiation of an unpredictable process. Arendt was most interested in the way that the principles of work had migrated into action, particularly the use of "the ends justify the means" in politics. The classic line of twentieth-century politics "to make an omelet you have to break a few eggs" led to Arendt's reply in the essay "The Eggs Speak Up." Arendt's point is that in politics, the realm of action, the ends are so unpredictable that they cannot justify the means, and more importantly the means tend actually to out-live and be more influential than the ends. This understanding of politics as work, the terms of fabrication over-riding those of action, is the foundation of both the administrative model of the most enlightened Western European regimes as well as power-politics of the less sympathetic ones.

At the risk of losing the thread, perhaps it can be observed that in the last hundred years, just as fabrication has taken over politics, and we are just the eggs to make the omelet, then the experience of the human capacity for action, spontaneity, real-time judgment, decision and execution has migrated out of politics, and become a central concern for cultural practice of all kinds. And so the stakes of that choreographer's denial of "improvisation" are perhaps higher than a technical distinction, and the implications of art as an event could have broader significance, stage a question of larger import. Without over-statement, it could be enough to say that this matrix of concerns is what grants such works their resonance and grasp upon us.

"...the epoch no longer simply demands a vague response to the question 'What is to be done?' ...it is now a question, if one wants to remain in the present, of responding to this question almost every week: 'What is happening?'"

– Guy Debord, *letter to Eduardo Rothe*, 1974

The image. Not only has the structure of fabrication extended into politics, but the organized use of image-making, and the seductiveness of symbols have transformed our public realm, leaving each of us, individually, unsure of what we see, perhaps even in the mirror, and certainly on the street, the parliament. In the last ten years even the most defined features have all the solidity of a face in the clouds.

These figures who populate Van Lankveld's work have more to do with drawing than painting. Taking up the principle of the sketch, in which all that is aimed for is the bare minimum line and shade needed to convey a figure or scene, these pictures, though entirely structured by their relation of process to finished work, remain in this way unfinished. Or, in other words, their mode of communication is more evocative than denotative, and offer us not only the space to wonder what figures might emerge from each paintings' smaller moments, but to sense without knowing quite why each quality of narrative and mood, the scene that is set by such faces, such girls, such limbs.

***Omen of the Day* – a rare landscape. Of course there is the subtext for the artist, but her reticence is judicious.**

Amidst the vast sea of all the not-knowing in my life, episodes can take on the quality of omens. I drove cross-country with a Mohawk woman who insisted that passing hawks were like signs from god – not positive or negative, good or bad luck – but rather like punctuation marks, to be recognized. The face of the ticket-checker on the tram, the sudden rain inescapable on the bicycle ride, the report from the doctor – do I have a daily omen, like my daily bread?

Omen for today – meaning held in abeyance. The question of signification and reception, recognition and reckoning is staged for us. Our daily due, our daily response, perhaps even our daily responsibility.

An episode defined by its beginning and end, in which we recognize what we can, identify with the funny face in the picture, like the one in the mirror. Process, and product. We, too, after all, will only get one shot at it. Hey, it could be worse.

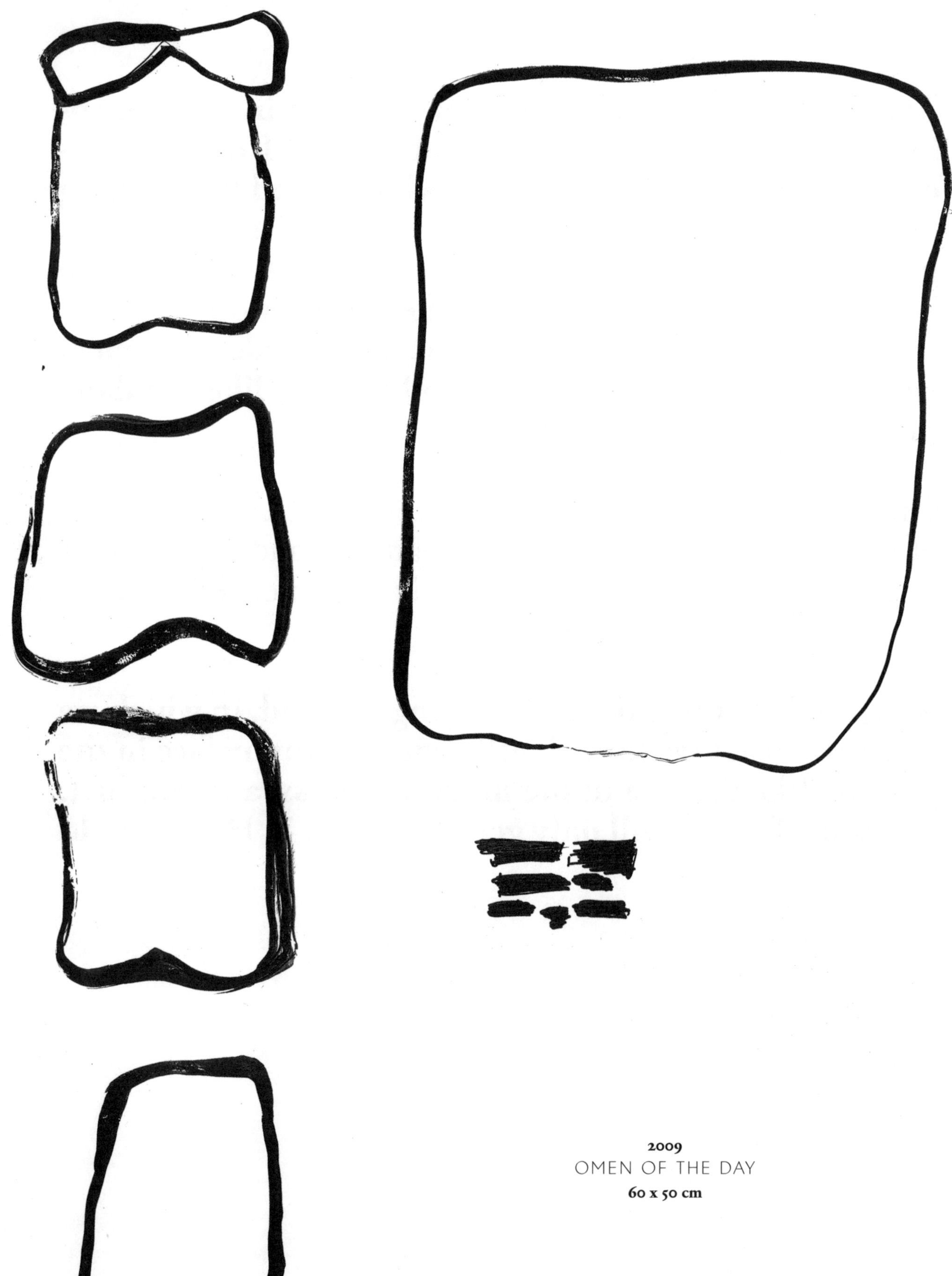

2009
OMEN OF THE DAY
60 x 50 cm

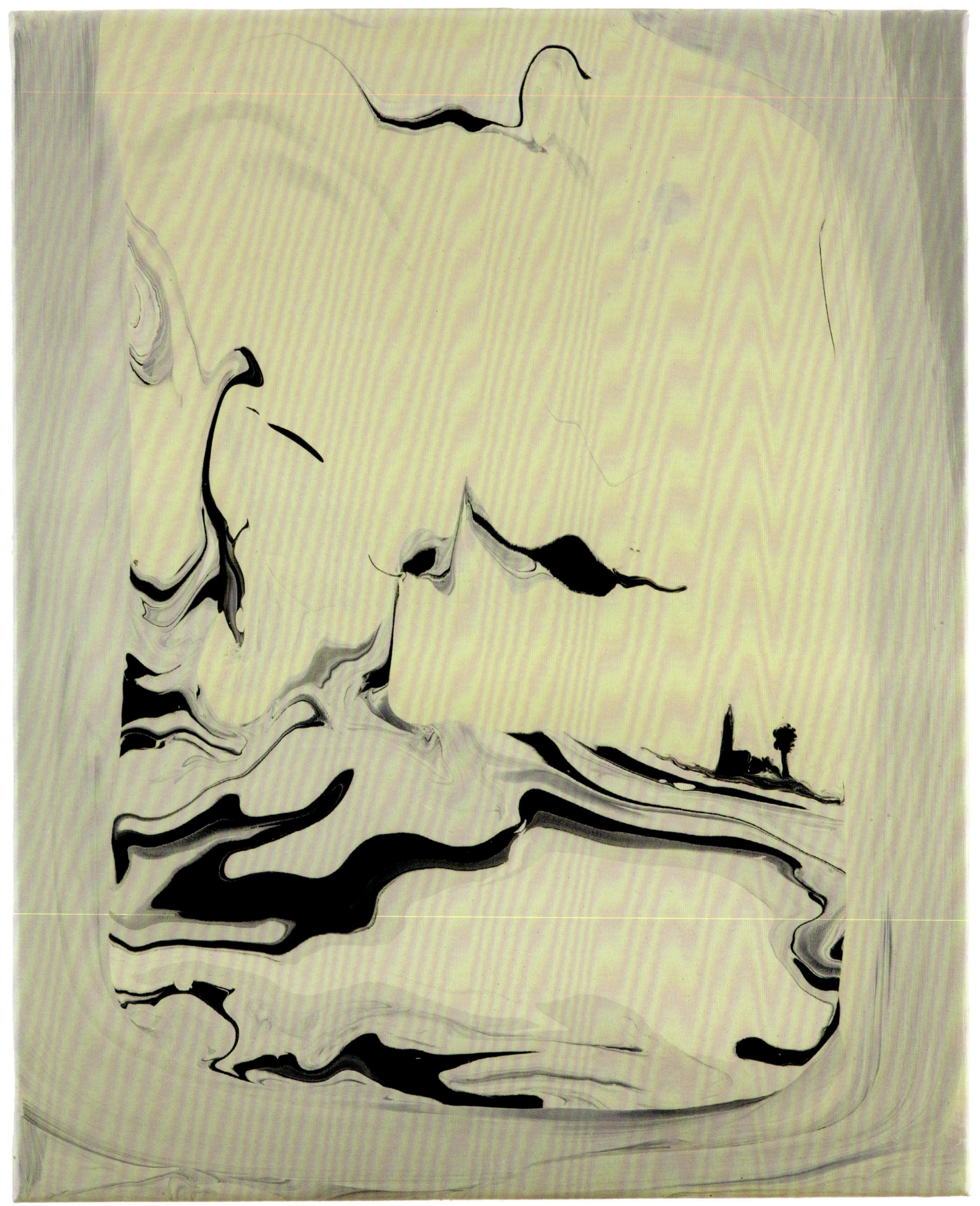

2009
SUBURBIA
125 x 110 cm

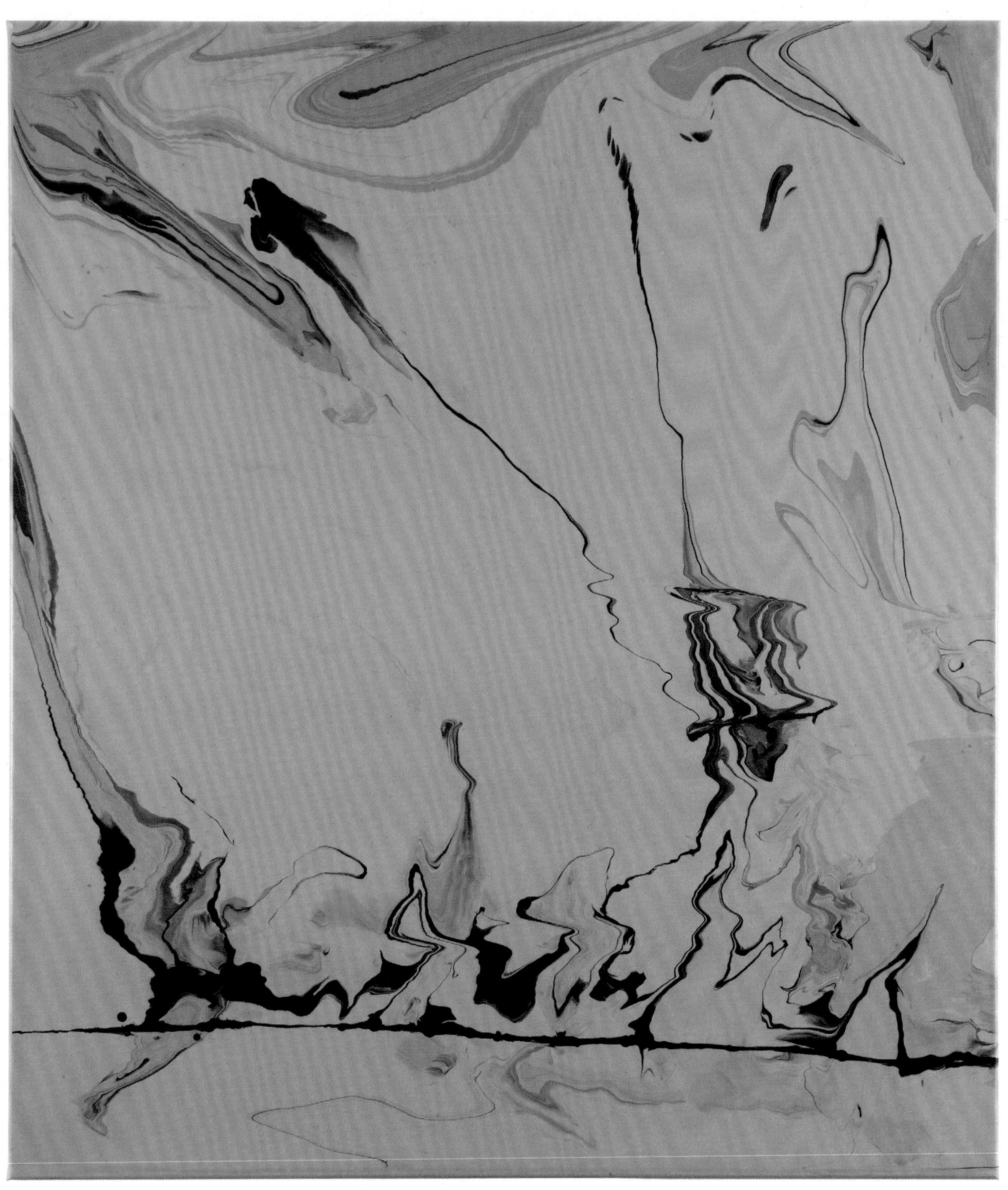

2009
UNTITLED (SPILLIAERT)
31 x 27 cm

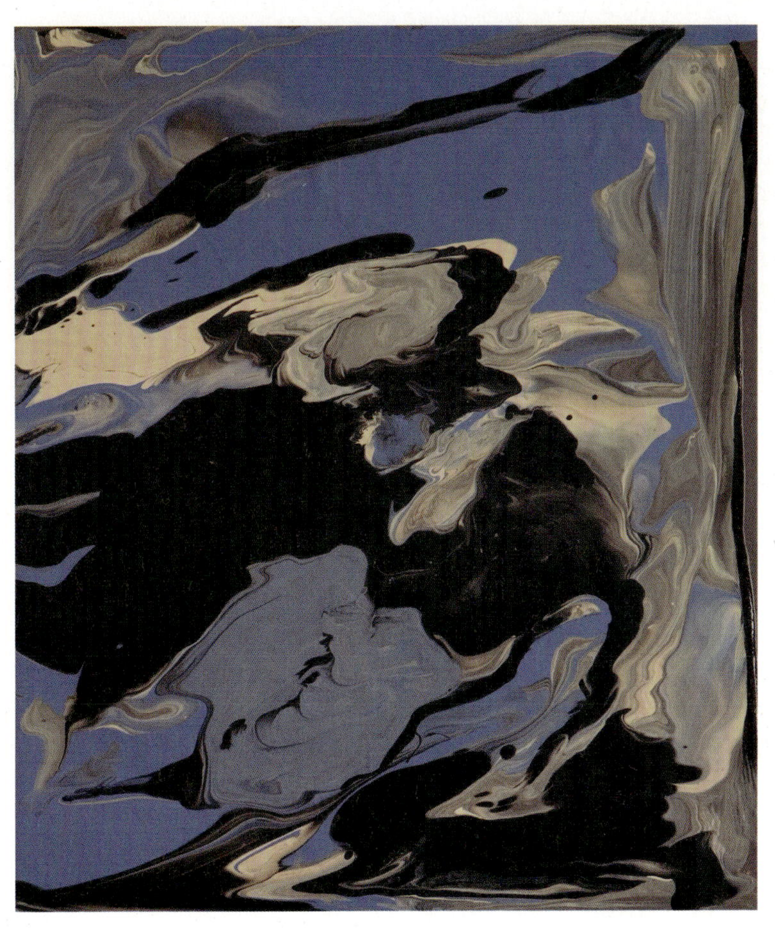

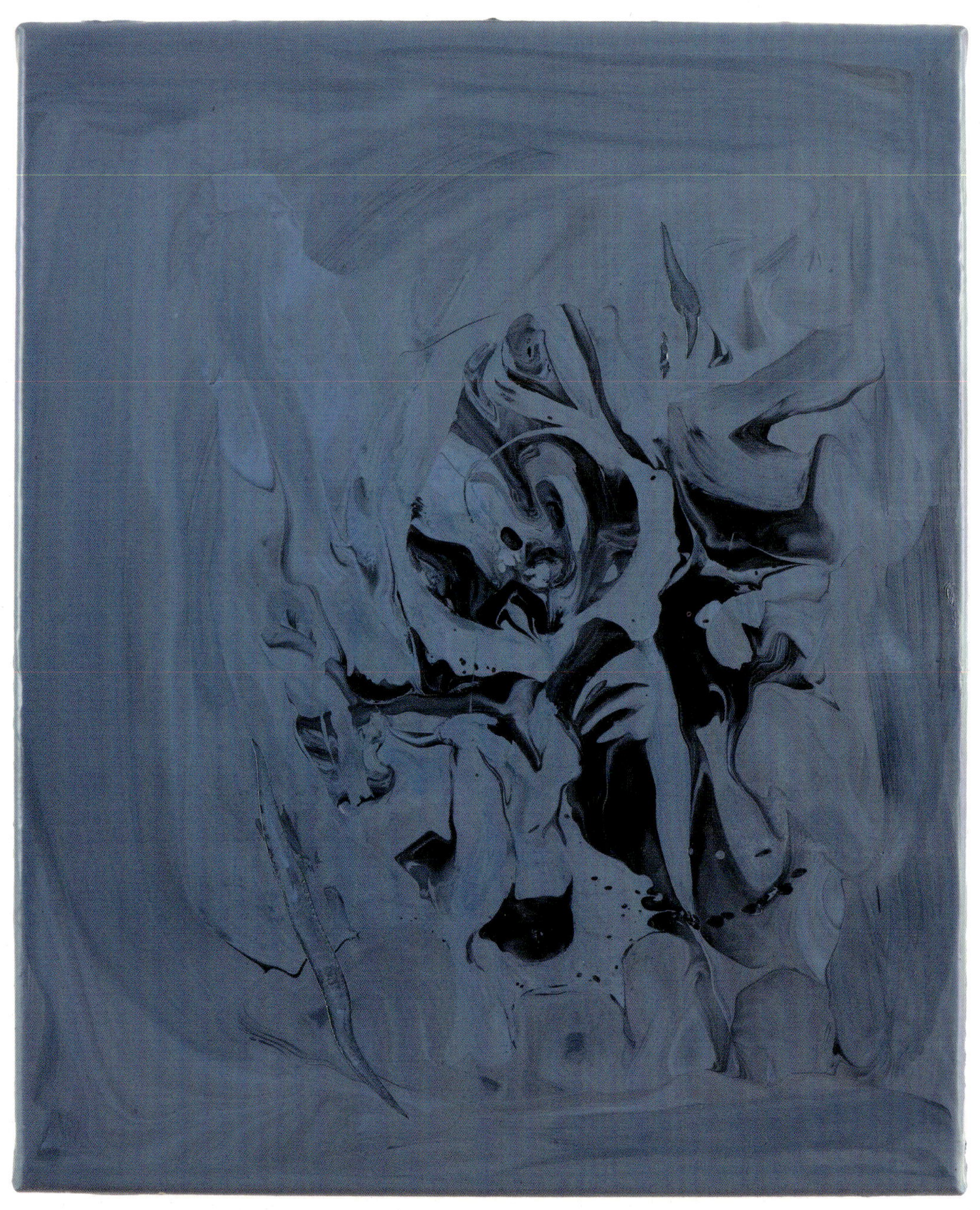

2009
NEST
60 x 50 cm

2009
MISI MOISY
65 x 50 cm

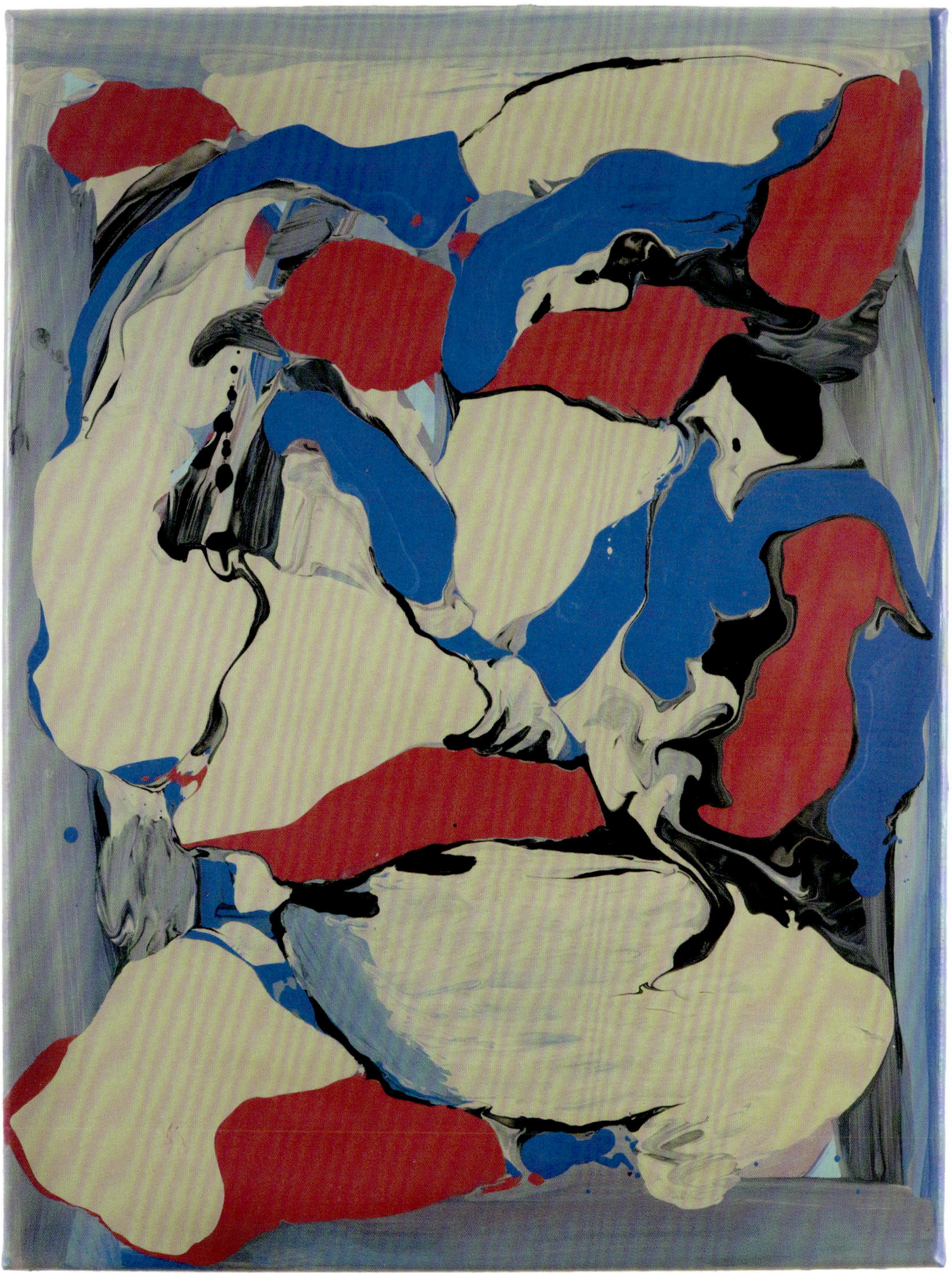

2009
SWAN
40 x 30 cm

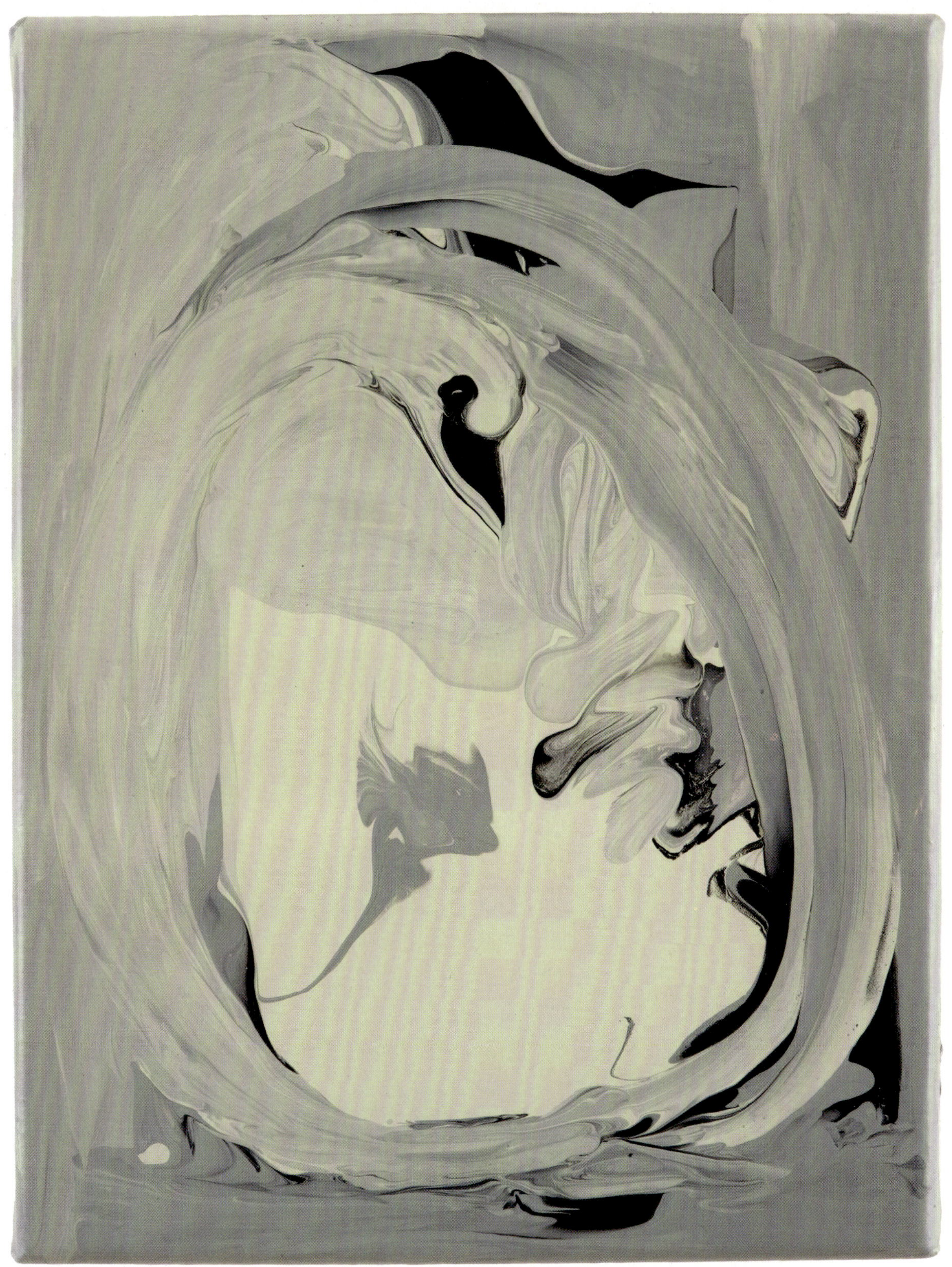

2009
XXXXXX
125 x 110 cm

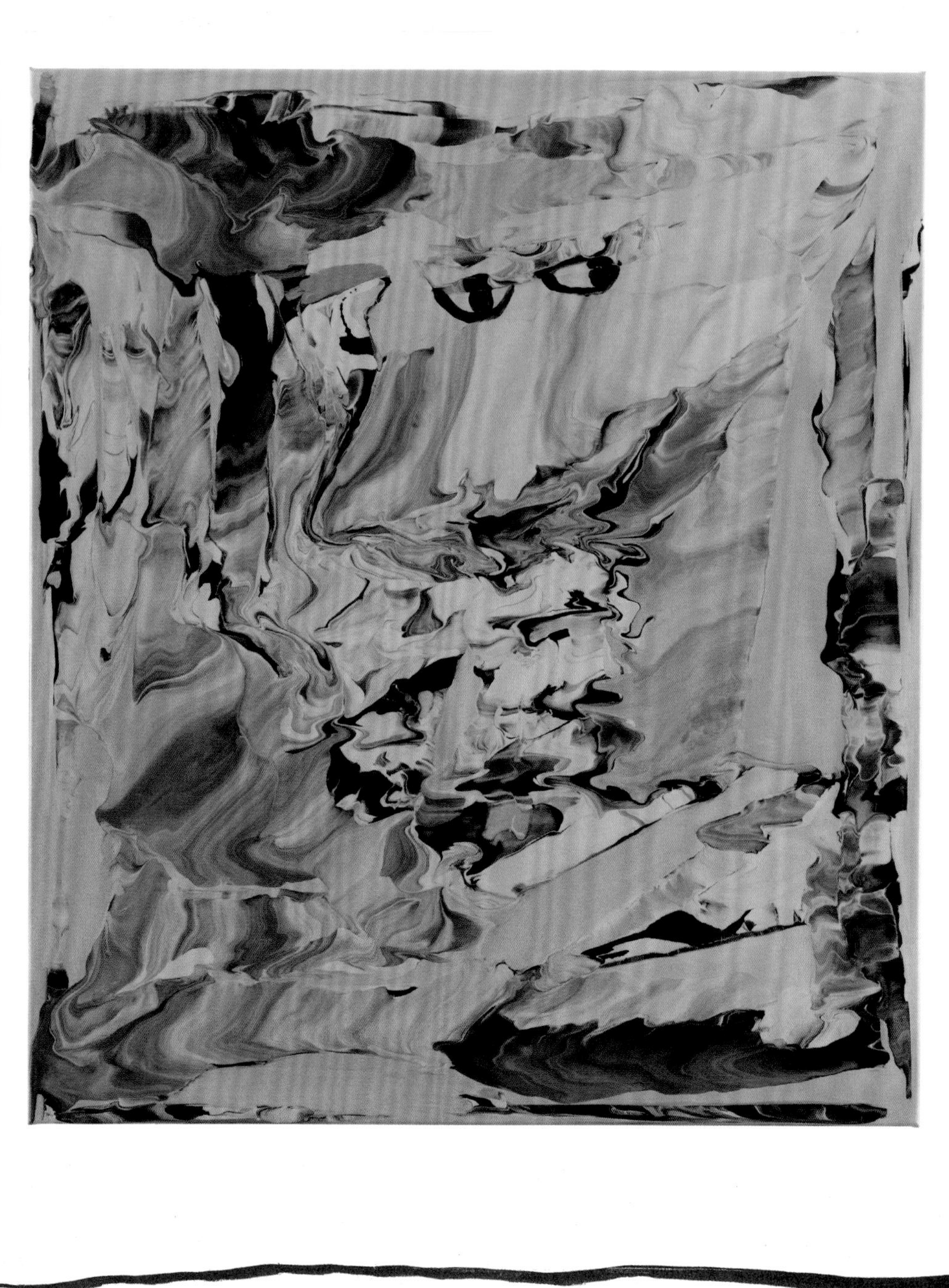

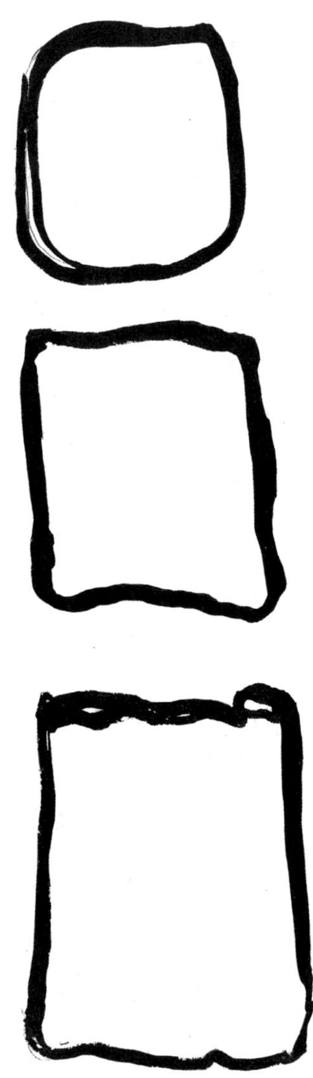

2010
LAZILY FAIRY
60 x 50 cm

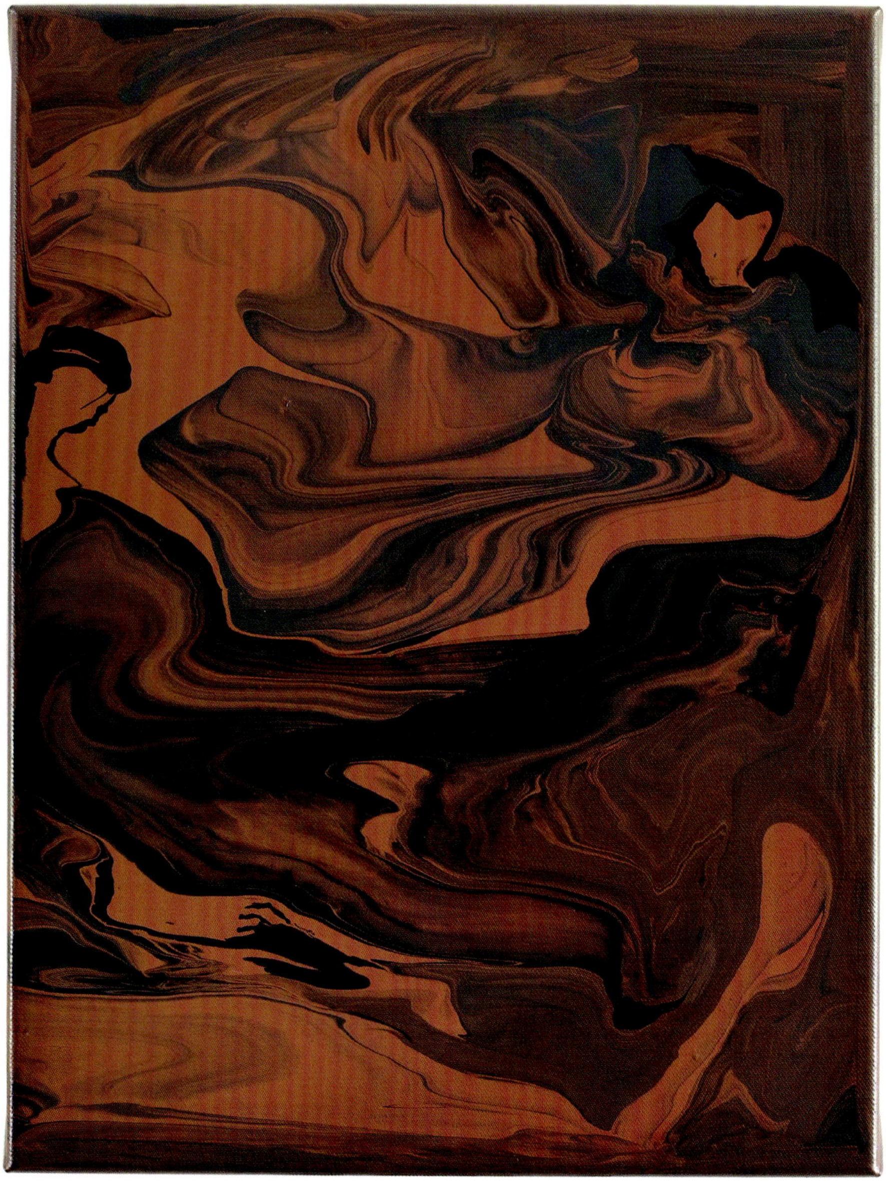

2010

HIJ KIJKT NAAR JOU

80 x 70 cm

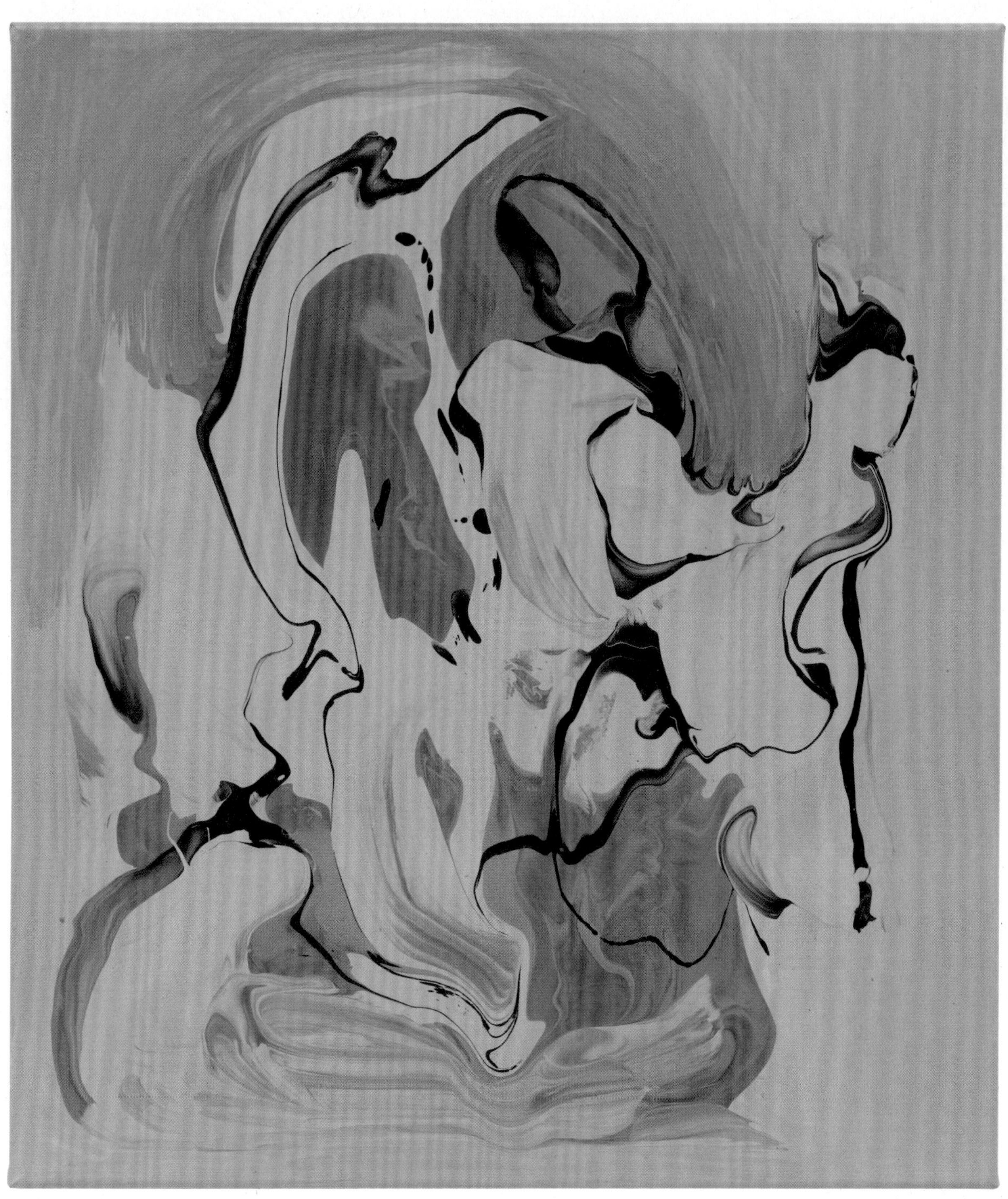

2010

ON THE PRAIRIE

120 x 120 cm

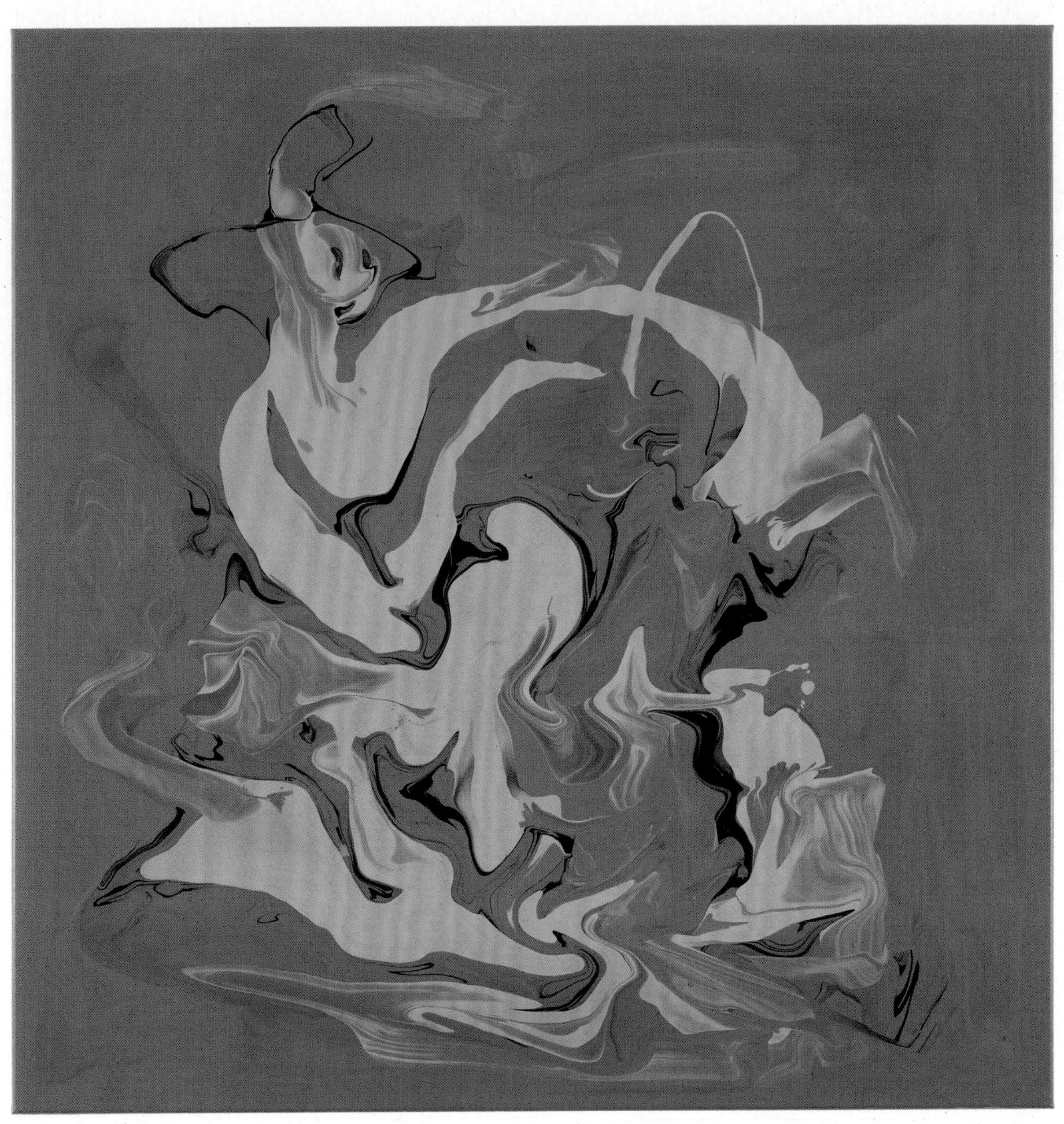

2010
CANNES
105 x 90 cm

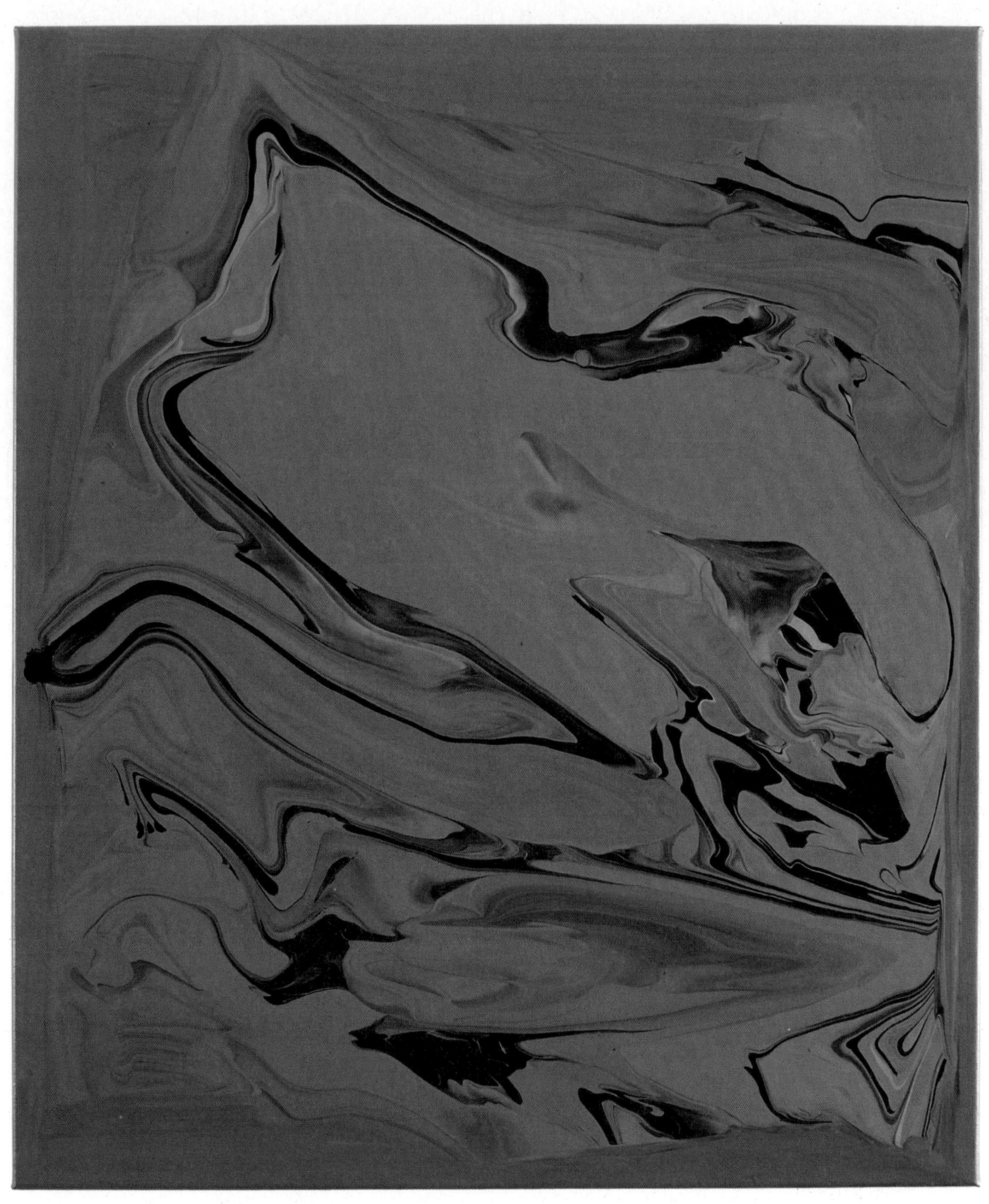

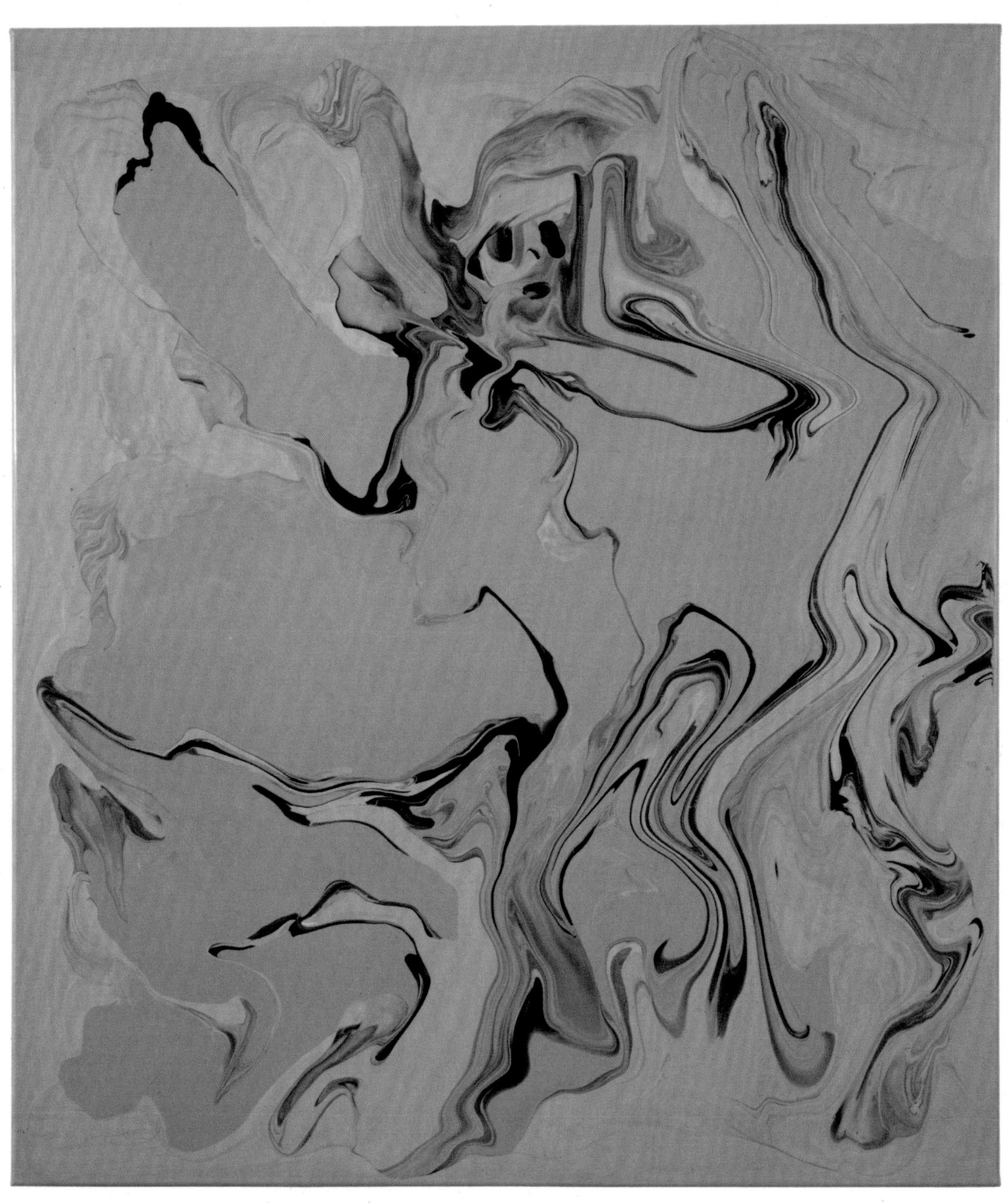

WRITING FIREFLIES
MELISSA GRONLUND

2010
HERO
125 x 110 cm

We are absurdly accustomed to the miracle of a few written signs being able to contain immortal imagery, involutions of thought, new worlds with live people, speaking, weeping, laughing. We take it for granted so simply that in a sense, by the very act of brutish routine acceptance, we undo the work of the ages, the history of the gradual elaboration of poetical description and construction, from the treeman to Browning, from the caveman to Keats. What if we awake one day, all of us, and find ourselves utterly unable to read?

– Vladimir Nabokov, *Pale Fire*

In Dr. Oliver Sacks's case study *The Man Who Mistook His Wife for a Hat*, he tells of someone with prosopagnosia, a neurological disorder in which men and women cannot recognize faces, even of those they know well. They fail to identify friends, wives and children, and are at times unable to recognize a person in the most basic sense. The subject of Sacks's study, for example, on getting up to greet the doctor walked towards a grandfather clock and attempted to shake its hand. In the doctor's office, he took hold of his wife's head and tried to set it upon his head. Sacks himself also suffers from this disorder; as he writes in a subsequent article, "Face Blindness", in *The New Yorker*, he once combed his beard in a mirror – until he learned the 'mirror' was another bearded man, looking at him in annoyance.

The chagrin and irritation, in cases of prosopagnosia, remains on the part of those around the person with the disorder. The afflicted sail merrily past their children and friends; they are at times embarrassed, but do not feel the deep discomfort a person without prosopagnosia might feel in a similar situation. For prosopagnosiacs this lack of recognition is as normal as an inability to read a foreign script. But for those who see legibility in all languages, as it were, the incapacity to distinguish people is frightening, as it implies not just a perceptual shortcoming but a cognitive one as well. It is a failure of comprehension and memory, two bulwarks out of which one creates a sense of self. It is into this emotionally and psychologically fraught field that Rezi van Lankveld's oil paintings – with their faces, forms and structures that seem to just barely emerge from the paintwork – enters. Hovering on the edge of recognisability, her figures stage the question of how one distinguishes elements and orients him or herself within the world – the satisfaction and surprise of recognition, but also the frustration and confusion of seeing only forms and colour. During the onset of Modernism, in the early twentieth century, the psychological implications of the move from representation to abstraction were a subject of live debate: Erwin Panofsky, famously, and others looked at abstraction to understand how the eye and the mind translate shapes into recognizable figures, that is, how the mind overrides gaps in information to "see" a figure, or how it draws on learned memory to "understand" a type of relation, such as that of a mother and son, where only shapes really exist. Van Lankveld's uncertain images revive this discussion, but focus on its processual qualities: what is the process of this recognition, and, perhaps more importantly, what is the affective dimension that accompanies it?

In thinking through this problem we might identify two temporalities of looking to go with the two categories of painting suggested above: the long duration of appreciation and understanding a work whose meaning is conveyed by the abutment of different forms and shapes, and the instantaneous recognition of a scene. Van Lankveld's flits between both, and in her work the second comes as a jolt, not just of recognition, but a surprise that the painting we thought we knew – the one concerned with its texture, colour and form – was in fact conspiring to *look back* at us, handing to us a vista in which we ourselves could be placed. For if abstraction suggests a visual expanse, representationality builds a field for the human subject, who recognizes the forms before him or her as indicative of a world he or she might exist in.

This is deliberately not clear-cut in Van Lankveld's work, as she problematizes the fact as well as the act of recognition. In *Hero* (2010; p.92) two eyes and a mouth peer uncertainly from the swathes of paint in; the outline of a body in *Hij kijkt naar jou* (*He's looking at you*, 2010; p.86) faces the viewer, as the title suggests – or perhaps glances over his shoulder – and perhaps does not exist at all. In *Omen of the Day* (2009; p.71) a small town, made of a tower and a group of buildings, perches improbably on a crest of pure paint. Can we be sure we are even seeing something – is it a trick of the paint, a mirage of the oil, a gimmick, even, pulling us out of abstraction? Though her work creates figures, these seem to belong to the paint itself rather than a human imaginary, and the ability to recognize these figures does not lend themselves to a figurative scene but a narrative stemming from her process, of how she made these works and how, or at what point, she stopped.

This performativity brings to mind a curious facet to Sacks's story of the man who mistook his wife for a hat. The man in question was a musicologist, and he supplanted his ability to recognize faces and useful objects with music as the ordering principle of daily routine: if he sang or hummed, he could eat a meal without difficulty. If he stopped singing, he would look at the fork in his hand and the people opposite him in confusion. When he picked up humming again, the free-floating shapes and forms about him would render up to him their function, and he could again begin eating with utensils and chatting to his wife and friends opposite. As his condition worsened, he began to hum or play the piano almost constantly, relying almost totally on the logic or sensibility internal to music to provide the comprehensibility to his day that visual recognition previously had.

Though trading one sense (vision) for another (sound), humming has the effect of making perceptible the act of looking – or, in this subject's case, replacing looking with another sensual process. (Certain, especially earlier, works of Van Lankveld also seems involved in directly mapping this attention or process, particularly in their impression of three-dimensionality. In works such as *Grey Man* (2009) and the suite of untitled works from 2001 to 2003, paint is added onto paint to make each figure, such that the paintings are materially – that is, they do not just represent – graphs of sites of activity.) Humming, to put it another way, dramatises the act of perception, turning what is often thought of as a result ("I see someone!") into a process, an act.

We might posit this fluid sensibility, or vision blending into music and movement, against the horror evoked by the narrator of Nabokov's *Pale Fire* in the excerpt quoted above, who fears not being able to decipher the biro-blue written script of the notecards he carries – but who also ultimately moves away from this dystopia towards soaring hopes for super-legibility, of being able to decode, for example, fireflies' writing "signals on behalf of stranded spirits" in the "bruised and battered" night sky. This performative understanding conceives of recognition as an act always in process, one in which recognition is not binary (yes, I see it/ no, I don't) and which brings painting far away from something whose task is to represent or replicate. Van Lankveld's works participate in a wider critique of "looking" that contemporary painters are exploring, not by focusing on the power politics of the gaze, but by rendering the process of looking as both emotionally and psychologically unfixed. If we cannot know how we see, how can we be sure what we see? Or are there alternate ways of engaging with paintings – as performative, as in the example of the humming prosopagnosiac, or as indefinite, an extended horizon that is never closed or contextualised? Moreover, in isolating representationality so that it is no longer a referent – her paintings are not landscape paintings or portraits – she hones in on the question of recognisability itself, and its unique connection to painting, whose historic task was to create things that we can, or cannot, recognize as resembling something else.

But concentrating too much on the figures ignores their background: the bruised and battered skies of non-recognition that linger, in two-dimensional non-space, behind the forms. The strong affectiveness of these colours and shapes conveys, perhaps, not just the fear of non-representationality but the joy of it as well – alternate ways of thinking and moving within and seeing the world, that are able to connect more directly to the emotions of the viewer than to the intellect of his or her comprehension. Let us see prosopagnosia not as a curse but as an opportunity.

2010
SYMPTOM
135 x 120 cm

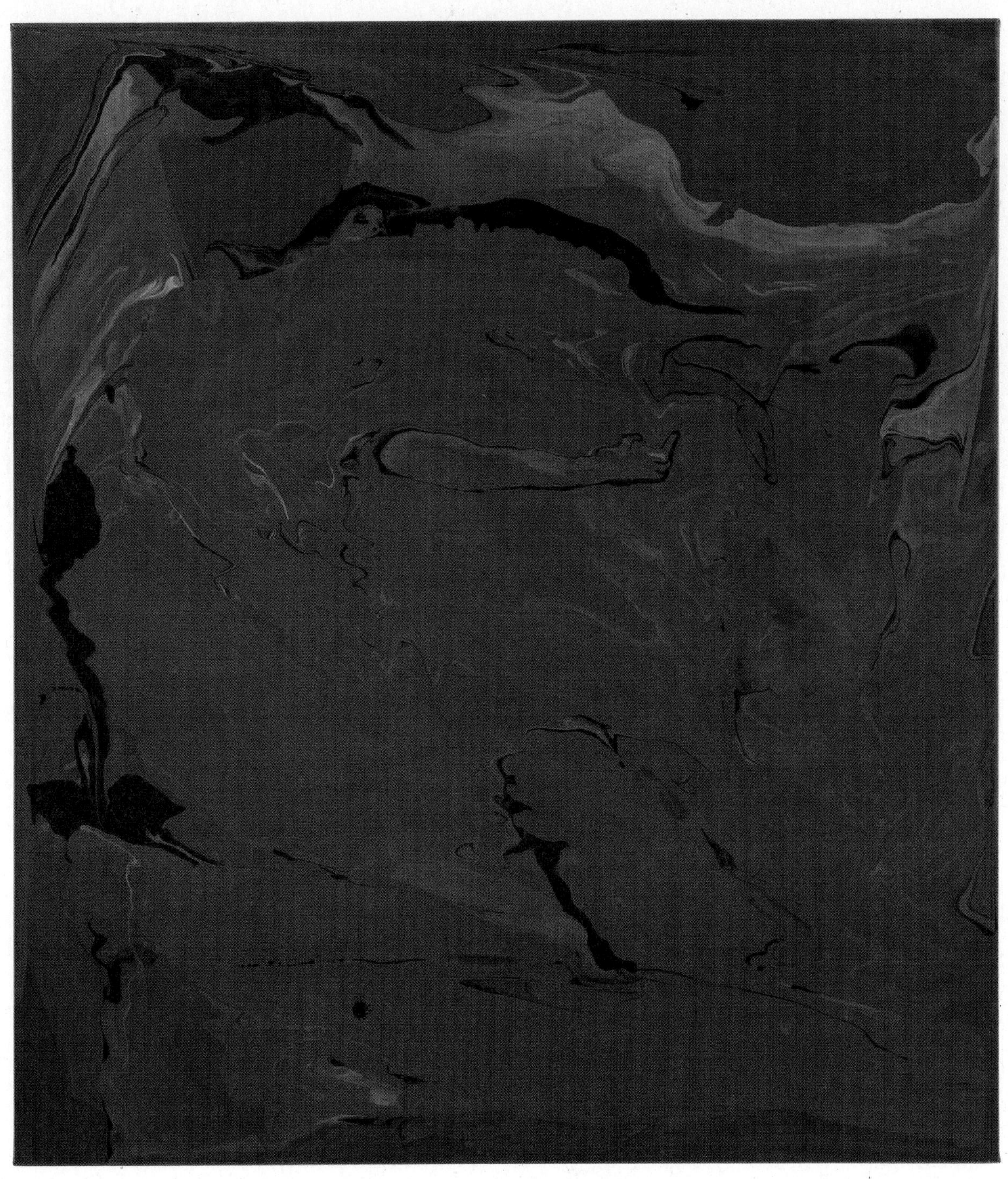

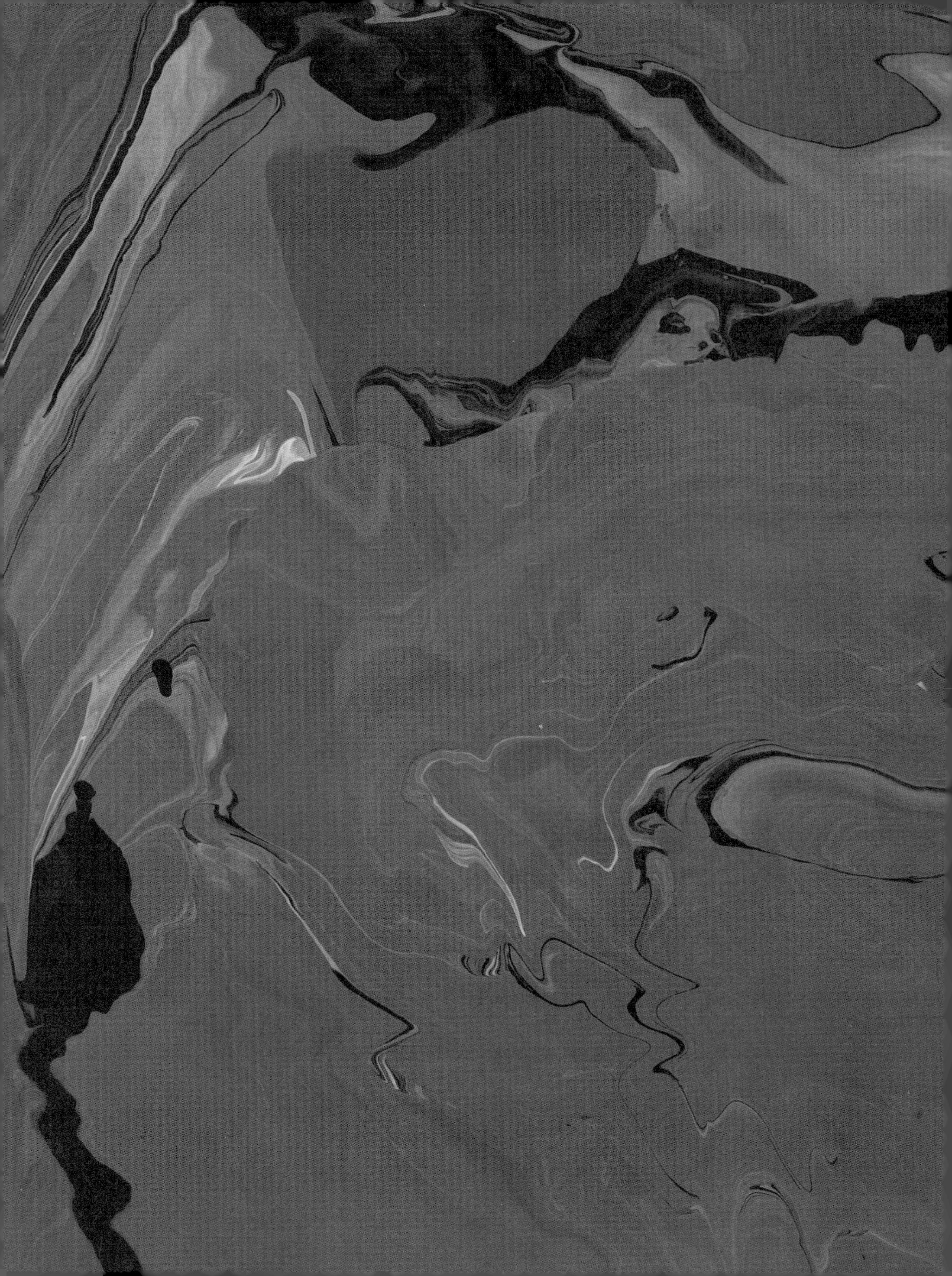

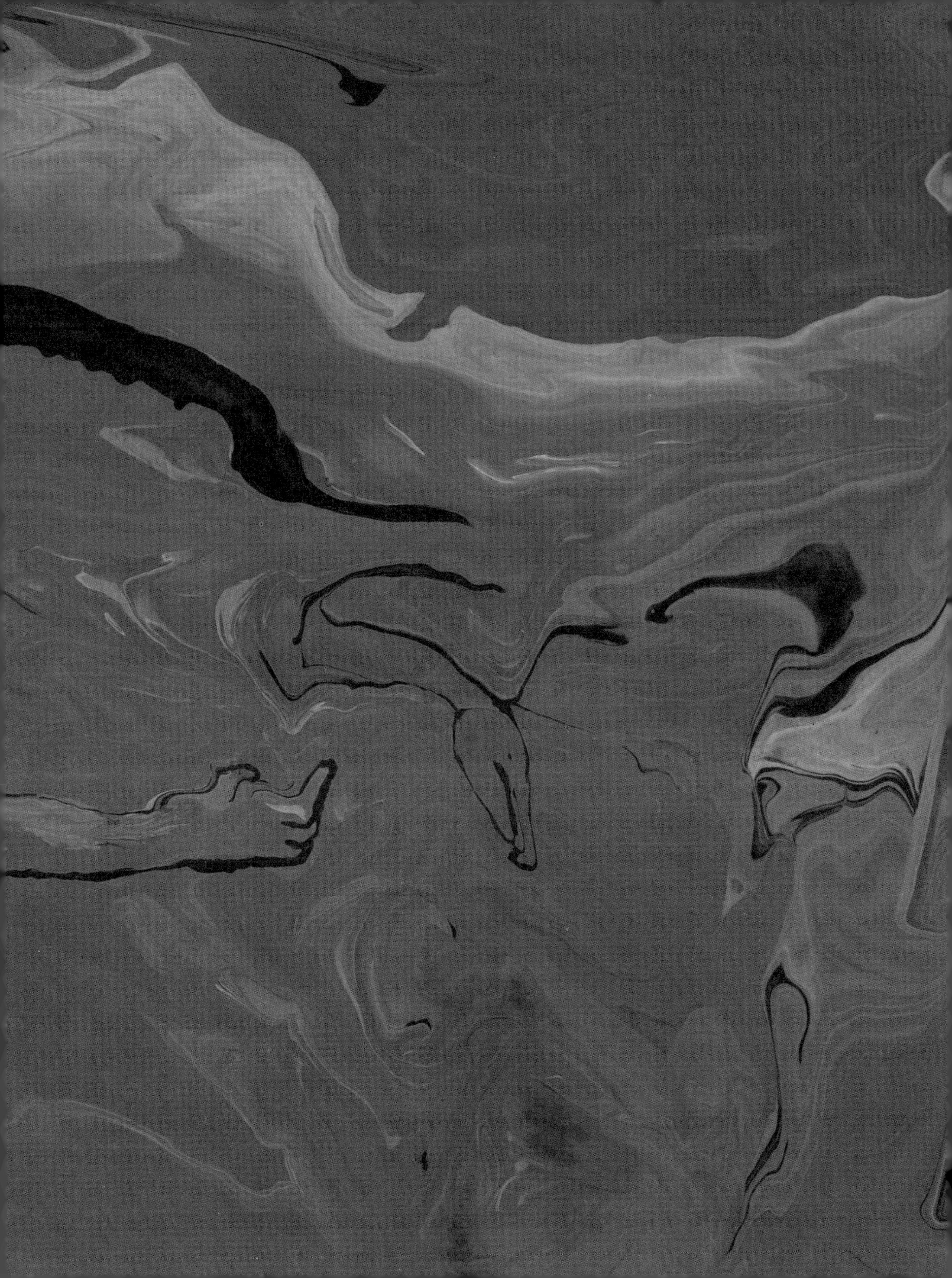

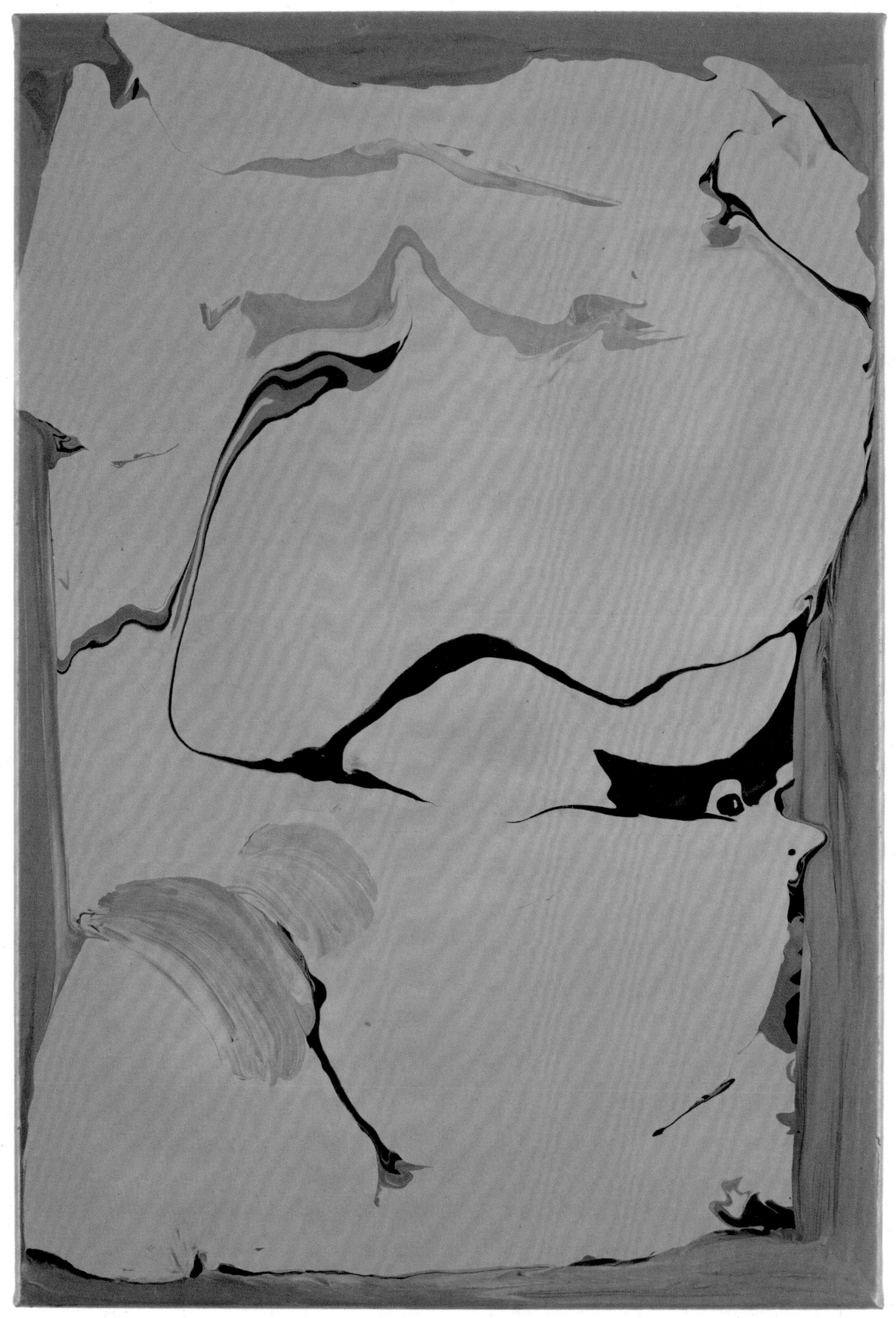

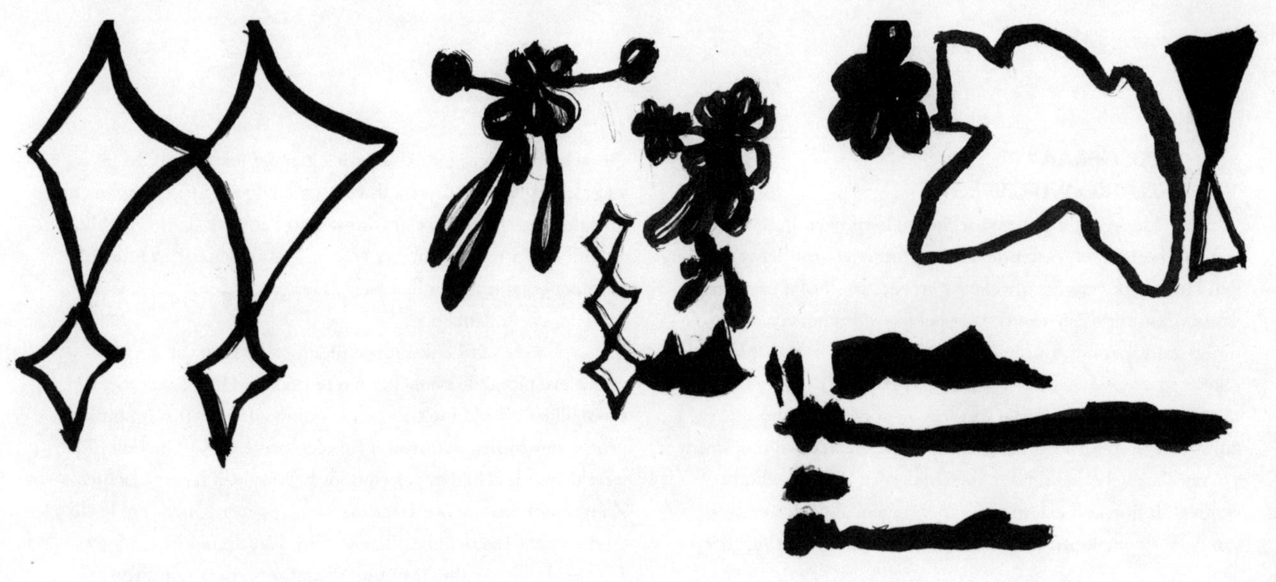

2010
MOUNTAIN OF ZORRO
80 x 56 cm

LOSGERAAKT
ZLATKO WURZBERG

Heel vaak wordt een schilderij besproken in termen van zijn voorbeeld, zijn referenties en de context waarin het verschijnt. Een kunstwerk verwijst ofwel naar vroeger voorbeeld ofwel naar de toeschouwer die het werk later bekijkt, alsof het een soort transparant medium is, een intermediair tussen deze disparate zaken.

Als wij kijken naar historische of hedendaagse kunstwerken met enige mate van figuratie, nemen wij nog steeds aan dat de afgebeelde figuren de schilderijen – die beschouwd worden als hun verbeeldingen – voorgingen, alsof de ervaring van de abstracte kunst deze gewoonte niet allang onderuit heeft gehaald.

Eeuwenlang waren wij geneigd een kunstwerk te zien als een reflectie of een representatie van de wereld. Bovenal van belang waren de inhoud, de details en de betekenis van de afgebeelde actie, naast de competentie van de kunstenaar in het uitdrukken van ideeën. Er werd aangenomen dat de oorsprong van elk kunstwerk gebaseerd was op inhoud (zoals een motief of een idee), wat voorop werd gesteld als de origine van een actie of een toekomstig werk.

In de lange modernistische periode ging het schilderen echter meer de kant uit van de zelfverwijzing. Net zoals bij andere kunsten was het schilderen begonnen aanspraak te maken op een specifiek competentiegebied, waarbij de aandacht gericht werd op het weergeven van zichzelf in een soort van intransitiviteit, en deze kwaliteit vervolgens verder uit te werken. Deze notie werd overtuigend verwoord door de Amerikaanse criticus Clement Greenberg: "De essentie van het modernisme ligt in mijn ogen in het gebruik van de karakteristieke methodes van een discipline om die discipline zelf te bekritiseren, niet om haar te ondermijnen, maar om haar steviger te verankeren in haar competentiegebied."

De schilderkunst is vervolgens teruggekeerd naar het weergeven van de buitenwereld. Toch tracht ze nu ook andere representaties van de wereld weer te geven, variërend van symbolische, fotografische en cineastische tot journalistieke en meer. Ze heeft zichzelf neergezet als een kunstmedium zonder traditie of, in het gunstigste geval, als een eerbetoon aan meesterschap (dit idee kan nog worden toegeschreven aan Edouard Manet).

Aan de andere kant zou men erop kunnen wijzen dat abstracte kunst een eerste daad van zelfoprichting en zelfcreatie vooronderstelt. De hypothese is dat deze daad zowel aanvangsmoment is (in de zin dat er niets aan voorafgaat) als precies die vonk die alles ontketent. Daarom is deze drijvende kracht het eerste kunstzinnige gebaar dat alle processen die het werk tot stand brengen bewerkstelligt. Het is niet slechts een uitvoerende kracht, maar wordt direct ingevoerd in het werk en is dan niet meer te onderscheiden van wat het tot stand brengt.

Omgekeerd is deze creatie identiek aan het gebaar zelf. In plaats van zichzelf te presenteren als een samenvloeiing van verschillende bronnen die tot uitdrukking komen in het werk, is er één enkele auteur. Het artistieke subject creëert vanuit zichzelf en is de absolute oorsprong van het werk. Het geschilderde beeld is aan niets anders te danken.

Rezi van Lankvelds schilderijen beogen van beelden exclusieve picturale evenementen te maken. Het beeld moet een duidelijke uitdrukking van zijn wording zijn: het rijst op uit het proces van zijn eigen vorming, als een projectie van de innerlijke wereld van de schilder, gezien door het oog van haar gedachten. Zonder ook maar iets extrinsieks weer te geven, opent het beeld de deur naar een denkbeeldige wereld. Het domein van Van Lankvelds verbeelding is nooit arbitrair en wordt ten diepste gedreven door de logica van haar manier van schilderen. Van meet af aan is duidelijk dat Rezi van Lankveld niet de intentie heeft om een (echte of denkbeeldige) wereld af te beelden of om een idee te illustreren. Dit kun je afleiden uit het feit dat ze elke picturale illusie en elke hint van realistische representatie die een soort kunstzinnig illusionisme zou kunnen veronderstellen, verwerpt. Het schilderij als zodanig moet zich in eerste instantie ontvouwen in zijn materialiteit, blootgelegd als kleur en verf, laag en penseeltoets, als hun beweging op het oppervlak, enzovoort. Het moet in staat zijn zijn eigen wereld te creëren. Hoewel deze schilderijen misschien doen denken aan "toevallig gemaakte beelden" (zoals bijvoorbeeld Leonardo's afgetakelde muren of Alexander Cozens' vlekkenschilderijen), zijn ze juist met grote opzet gemaakt.

Vanaf het allereerste begin streeft de schilder naar een beeld: zij wil een beeld produceren dat uit zichzelf al een integraal onderdeel is van het werkproces en dat geen beginmodel heeft dat getransformeerd, onderworpen en uiteindelijk door het schilderij verloochend moet worden. De visuele componenten die worden geproduceerd door het schilderproces tellen niet samen op tot een uiteindelijk geheel. Het beeld bestaat op hetzelfde niveau als alle andere materiële elementen, vervlochten in de ambiguïteit van de vorm. Alleen ontdekt men hier niet de gebruikelijke tegenstelling die het beeld reduceert tot pure vormen, alsof het om een abstractie gaat, of tot een figuratieve representatie. Zo hoeft onze blik niet te kiezen om te kijken naar het beeld of naar het schilderij. Binnen de ruimte van zo'n werk hoeft de blik niet heen en weer te bewegen tussen de naakte manifestatie van de schilderkunst enerzijds en haar figuren anderzijds, alsof die twee zienswijzen tegenover elkaar zouden staan. Zulke schilderijen zouden met andere woorden niet worden geïnterpreteerd volgens Richard Wollheims these van de tweevoudigheid van het 'zien in' en het gelijktijdige besef van wat is afgebeeld en van de afbeelding, van het subject en het medium. Bovendien is de kijkervaring van het 'zien in', zoals belichaamd door de bekende eend/konijn-figuur, ook niet van toepassing. Er is een continu besef dat je naar

een schilderij kijkt: je hebt nooit de illusie dat je naar iets kijkt
wat op een afbeelding lijkt. Het bekijken van het schilderij is
enkelvoudig; dit is waar de imaginaire ervaring om draait.

Het schilderij haalt zijn kracht uit de spanning tussen de
daad van het schilderen en het beeld, wat zijn inhoud genoemd
kan worden, maar slechts ten dele. Beeld wordt niet afgezet tegen
materie: hun relatie is dynamisch. Ze vindt plaats binnen een
ruimte waar alles op al het andere kan inwerken, of iets anders kan
worden. Die beelden kunnen verwijzen naar de popcultuur of de
kunstgeschiedenis, naar privémotieven en gemoedstoestanden of
vluchtige situaties. Juist deze heterogeniteit kan je in de verleiding
brengen om ze – foutief – te zien als metabeelden die de essentie
van het schilderij tonen, of een bepaalde attitude tegenover de
visualiteit zelf: het beeld zou zo overkomen als een reflectie op het
schilderij van waaruit het werd geproduceerd. Het picturale beeld
is noch de inhoud van het schilderen noch schilderen als inhoud:
het is hun intermediair, het is juist de omschakeling en het
punt waarop instabiele figuren vorm krijgen in de altijddurende
verstrengeling tussen de verbeelding van de kijker en de realiteit
van het schilderij.

Rezi van Lankveld schildert in continue onzekerheid,
waarbij elk gebaar van de schilder een nieuwe beslissing vergt.
Als schilderen beschouwd moet worden als een continu proces
van besluiten nemen, dan komt dat zonder twijfel door de
verscheidenheid aan richtingen die men kan inslaan, afhankelijk
van de bestaande referentiepunten binnen een bepaald schilderij
– en ook omdat geen van deze richtingen a priori gekozen is. De
gegeven referentiepunten komen voort uit het schilderen, niet uit
zintuiglijke stimuli van de buitenwereld. Geen enkele beslissing
is een must, aangezien de keuze die gemaakt moet worden nooit
wordt voorgedragen en al zeker niet wordt voorgeschreven – maar
het is juist deze keuzevrijheid die keuzes noodzakelijk maakt.
Geen keuze maken betekent alle hoop op het beeld laten varen.
Foutieve of onbevredigende keuzes resulteren in niet-overtuigende
schilderijen die de kunstenaar zal uitwissen – en dan begint het
schilderspel van voren af aan. Het lijkt bijna alsof Van Lankveld
niet aan het schilderen was, alsof ze haastig vormen silhouetteert in
natte vernis, en met hun omtrekken improviseert. In feite schildert
zij nooit een beeld: zij anticipeert een beeld, zoals een voyeur die
op de loer ligt, in de hoop op een begeerde scène. Het is minder
belangrijk iets te zien dan te geloven dat iets gezien kan worden.

Het medium waarin Van Lankveld schildert is vloeibaar
maar onbestendig en het biedt geen ruimte voor lange pauzes
in het proces. Een sessie moet zonder pauze afgemaakt worden.
De kunstenaar gebruikt haar penseel om esthetische vormen te
modelleren in natte, zeer dik aangebrachte lagen verf. Maar in
plaats van de impastokwaliteit van olie- of acrylverf, heeft de
oppervlakte van haar schilderij een frescoachtige droogte. Ditzelfde
geldt voor de kleuren: het zijn niet alleen homogene kleurtinten,
maar ze zijn ook nog getemperd en gedempt, neigend naar

grisaille – in sterk contrast met primaire kleuren. Schakeringen
overlappen, sijpelen over het oppervlak, gaan vrij allerlei kanten
op of worden door het penseel vloeiend geleid, wat doet denken
aan gouache. Het grootste deel van het oppervlak is deels of geheel
bedekt door verf. De penseelstreek – beurtelings constructief en
beschrijvend of nerveus en beverig, maar altijd licht – definieert
nooit een complete vorm. Nooit te zien als geheel, alleen ten dele,
of als een hint, creëren de vormen een oppervlak in een ritmische
beweging. Het schilderij vindt zijn dynamische balans in het
beeld: het beeld is het referentiepunt waarop de ogen van de kijker
kunnen vertrouwen, en waar het werk zijn essentie uit haalt. Wat
betreft hun compositie tonen de meeste schilderijen een golvend,
circulair ritme, net als rimpelingen in het water nadat er een steen
in is gegooid. (Esthetisch gezien zou de analogie van een zwevend
gordijn, uit de traditionele schilderkunst, het dichtst bij komen.
In de klassieke theorieën over het schilderen was de schoonheid
van een gordijn een grijs gebied waar de technische regels van het
schilderen tekortschoten, onderuitgingen of niet geldig bleken
– en toch was er een volmaakte bekwaamheid voor nodig. Een
dergelijke suggestie van beweging gaf het schilderij een temporele
dimensie die het dramatiseerde en de illusie van leven wekte.)

In dit overzicht van Rezi van Lankvelds werk zou men
geneigd kunnen zijn een evolutie te zien in de vorming van
beelden, van een tafereel waarin men verscheidene figuren zou
kunnen ontwaren, een soort schouwspel, tot een figuratieve
indicatie van een houding, een uitdrukking of een emotionele
staat, zoals een nieuwsgierige blik of onverschilligheid – een
specifieke contour van mensen, dingen, landschappen, enzovoort.
Hier onthult het beeld zichzelf als een knoop, een schets, een
wazige vlek. De kunstenaar toont het liever als een knoop dan het
te willen uitleggen en uitwerken tot alle ambiguïteit is verdreven
en we het beter kunnen begrijpen. Deze knoop is een hybride
lichaam, een brij van zich eigen gemaakte gebruiken, modellen
en observaties. Niets in deze schilderijen voelt transparant of
onschuldig, neutraal of een geheel – op het niveau van wat is
geschilderd of op het niveau van het beeld. Dat zou weer kunnen
memoreren aan Milan Kundera's beeld van het "magisch gordijn
opgehangen voor de wereld", als een kant-en-klaar pre-concept,
een pre-interpretatie van de wereld die aan het gezicht wordt
onttrokken. Volgens Kundera streeft de literatuur ernaar om dat
gordijn niet te verwarren met de wereld daarachter, maar om het
weg te rukken en de wereld in al haar naaktheid te onthullen.
Kunnen de beelden van bepaalde houdingen, gerecyclede
symbolen en andere figuren die worden waargenomen in de
schilderijen van Rezi van Lankveld dus niet worden opgevat als
kopieën van die fabels die geweven staan in het gordijn van de pre-
interpretatie? Misschien wel – mits je ze dan ook ziet als een vorm
die identiek is aan het wegrukken van dat gordijn.

DE GESCHILDERDE DRUPPEL
LEEN BEDAUX

Existentialistische vraagstukken leiden in de schilderijen tot een paradox. De sfeer die de taferelen uitstralen doet denken aan het onbezorgde leven van de negentiende-eeuwse bohémien, terwijl de onderwerpen die erin ter sprake komen juist uiterst urgent en verontrustend zijn. De negentiende-eeuwse bohémien gelooft onvoorwaardelijk in de ontplooiing van artistieke individualiteit en originaliteit, en is bereid er alles voor op te geven. Opwaaiende jurken, picknicktaferelen, romantische entredeuxs geplaatst in dromerige landschappen roepen vooral de idealen van de nonchalante bohémien op en tegelijkertijd worden deze idealen overladen door een monstrueus onheilspellend drama.

Deze paradox heeft ook een mediumspecifieke betekenis. Rezi van Lankveld benadert de idealen van de bohémien niet alleen in de taferelen, maar ook in haar meesterlijke materiaalbeheersing. Door quasi-argeloos de rijkdom van haar virtuositeit in te zetten, stelt ze deze demonstratief boven andere kwaliteiten zoals scholing, intellectuele vorming of functionaliteit. Ze beroept zich nadrukkelijk op artistieke individualiteit en daarmee op autonome kunstbeoefening. Toch is ze zich ervan bewust dat het ideaal van de negentiende-eeuwse bohémien botst met de maatschappelijke werkelijkheid, maar juist deze botsing is essentieel voor het begrip van schilderkunst van vandaag.

In de schilderijen zit een moralistische boodschap verborgen die contemplatie en beheersing opeist ten tijde van permanent accelererende mobiliteit en distributie. Onze samenleving wordt voortgedreven door een obsessieve veranderingsdrift. Continue uitdagingen om ergens in te geloven en ergens bij te horen bepalen het leefklimaat: altijd incompleet en nooit af, bezig met permanente identiteitsveranderingen, actief binnen sociale netwerken. De condities in de 21ste eeuw veranderen permanent en zo snel dat de mens er niet meer in slaagt deze te consolideren in gewoonten en routines. Het lijkt niet mogelijk om de enorme snelheid van verandering te vertragen, laat staan om haar richting te bepalen of te controleren.

Wij leven niet meer in duidelijk afgebakende gemeenschappen met duidelijke regels, maar in een tijdperk waarin niets nog duurzaam lijkt en waarin alles op ieder moment door iedereen onderhandelbaar is. Van Lankveld refereert in haar schilderijen zowel aan de klassieke traditie van de schilderkunst als aan specifieke (post)modernistische twistpunten. De hamvraag is hier of beeldende kunst nog wel iets in te brengen heeft als alle definieerbare kaders tot het verleden behoren en ook (tijd)-ruimtelijke parameters niet meer toereikend zijn. Kan een kunstwerk nog een definitieve gestalte krijgen als alles voordurend aan verandering onderhevig is? Deze en andere vragen lijken expliciet aan de orde te komen.

VLOEIBARE MODERNITEIT (LIQUID MODERNITY)

Het vluchtige is het kenmerk van de huidige tijd, volgens de Poolse socioloog Zygmunt Bauman, die sinds de jaren tachtig van de vorige eeuw over ontwikkelingen binnen de hedendaagse westerse samenleving schrijft. Met het modernisme werd een toekomst voorspeld die vrij zou zijn van de grillen van de natuur en haar vernietigende rampen, een toekomst zonder angst en onzekerheid. Echter heeft het moderne tijdperk niet ertoe geleid de natuur en haar grillen volledig te kunnen beheersen, erger nog, door menselijk toedoen staan we nu nog meer blootgesteld aan wereldbedreigende catastrofes. Bauman stelt dat onzekerheid, ongerustheid en vrees kenmerkend zijn voor de vloeibare moderniteit.

Vloeibare moderniteit staat tegenover vaste moderniteit. De vaste moderniteit is geworteld in de materiële wereld, houdt vast aan verlichte of religieuze waarden met een hang naar sociale utopieën. Vloeibare moderniteit daarentegen is pragmatisch en alleen als het uitkomt worden historische ankers uitgegooid, maar een echte geworteldheid ontbreekt. Dit zorgt voor grote instabiliteit en onzekerheid, maar geeft grote speelruimte met veel keuzemogelijkheden. Het is een tijdperk waarin mensen in hoog tempo afwegingen maken en telkens nieuwe besluiten nemen. Bauman schetst daarvoor een nieuw type: de kiezende mens, ofwel de *homo eligens*.

De schilderijen vertonen in het maakproces een analogie met deze vloeibare moderniteit. Onbeheersbare krachten van de vloeibare verf, zoals de effecten van zwaartekaart, het uitwaaieren van magere olieverf, reliëf en kleurdiepte bepalen in grote mate het beeld van de schilderijen. Deze veelheid aan simultane materiaalprocessen leveren een oneindig reservoir aan beelden die continu een besluit vragen om wel of niet in te grijpen. Vertrekkende vanuit een vormloze vloeibare massa wordt de verf door de maker gestuurd, figuraties doemen op uit een ondefinieerbaar veld van materie. Een kleine ingreep kan de verfmassa van richting doen veranderen en een geheel andere figuratie doen bovendrijven.

Het is niet de kiezende mens ofwel de *homo eligens*, maar de scheppende mens die de regie in handen heeft. Het maakproces wordt op een zeker moment stilgelegd en het resultaat wordt al dan niet geaccepteerd waarbij de laatste handeling van de kunstenaar beeldbepalend is. Deze laatste hand is op zijn minst een poging om de chaos, ofwel de catastrofe van onbeheersbare krachten, in te dammen en te controleren. De beslissing om een resultaat wel of niet te aanvaarden wordt dus enkel gemaakt door de kunstenaar. In het definitieve besluit van de kunstenaar dat het schilderij af is, ligt in zekere mate een fundamenteel geloof in de maakbaarheid. De beeldende kunst, of specifieker schilderkunst met vaste referentiepunten, overtuigt hiermee nog altijd zeggingskracht te hebben.

DE GESCHILDERDE DRUPPEL

Een nadere beschouwing van het schilderij *Tears* (2009)
kan hier verhelderend zijn. Dit schilderij maakt deel uit van een
serie schilderijen die in mindere mate de negentiende-eeuwse
bohémien oproepen, maar daarentegen bewust of onbewust meer aan
detwintigste-eeuwse schilderkunst refereren, zoals aan *De schreeuw*
van Edvard Munch, het expressieve schildersgebaar van Willem de
Kooning of de zwanen en ogen* van René Daniëls. Ook al liggen deze
kunsthistorische verwijzingen er niet dik bovenop, en zijn misschien
niet eens met opzet aangebracht, toch vormen ze een immanent
component van de beeldopbouw.

Wat hier aan de hand is, is dat de schilderijen door kleine
referenties het gewicht van deze traditie met zich meedragen. In mindere mate wordt hier de kunstzinnige levensvorm van de bohémien
geïdealiseerd. De sfeer van het negentiende-eeuwse kunstenaarsleven
heeft plaatsgemaakt voor een rationelere beeldopbouw met een
aantal subtiele verwijzingen naar specifieke schilderkunsticonen.
Deze verwijzingen benadrukken meer een verlangen naar de klassieke
schilderstraditie dan naar een uitbundige, artistieke levenssfeer.

Misschien is het daarom dat de geschilderde druppel,
ofwel de traan, in het schilderij *Tears* ergens doet denken aan de
parel van het meisje in het schilderij van Johannes Vermeer uit
1665-1667. In eenzelfde klassieke verhouding van de gulden
snede is de druppel hier op het canvas aangebracht. Evenals de
parel is de druppel met enkele penseelstreken trefzeker neergezet.
Een overeenkomstig hoog licht wijst bij de parel op het glansrijke
vormvaste oppervlak en bij de druppel op een transparante
vloeibare materie. Dus vaste en vloeibaar vorm staan hierin
opvallend dicht bij elkaar.

Het schilderij is daarmee bewust of onbewust geworteld
in de kunstgeschiedenis. Of algemener gezegd, er wordt veel
waarde gehecht aan het vasthouden van wortels. Het gaat niet
om vrijblijvende referenties, niet om een postmoderne spielerei
waarin de authenticiteit van andere schilders ondermijnd zou
worden, maar om een diepgeworteld geloof in de schilderkunst.
Het is dus geenszins een postmoderne ontvreemding, maar veel
meer spreekt uit dit schilderij een onlosmakelijke verbondenheid
met de scheppende mens. Het werk houdt dus zowel moderne als
postmoderne interpretaties binnenboord.

In de druppel ontspint zich een dichotomie van het
zijn en de representatie ervan, die in de vloeibaarheid van verf
en de geschilderde vorm van de druppel tot uitdrukking komt.
Door de clichématige vormgeving van de druppel is deze vooral
plat symbool zonder emotionele lading. Het is een pictogram
dat representatief staat voor de nat-in-nattechniek en de analogie
met vloeibare moderniteit. De geschilderde druppel steekt zo
fel af tegen de rest van het schilderij dat doordrongen is van een
schilderkunstige gelaagdheid die zich als een onmiddellijke en
rechtstreekse esthetische ervaring aandient.

* In het schilderij *De geamuzeerde muze*, 1983.

De nauwkeurig geplaatste detailleringen verleiden de kijker
om het verhaal erachter verder te doorgronden. De sensualiteit
van materie en materiaalbehandeling gaan naadloos over in
de sensualiteit van de figuratie. De sensatie ligt in het wel of
niet vinden van figuraties die doelbewust in een instabiele
balans worden gehouden. Het is alsof de soms wel en soms niet
opdoemende figuraties de spot drijven met het pathos van de
schilderkunst en zwaarbeladen analogieën, maar tegelijkertijd kan
er geen sprake zijn van spot, omdat de schilderkunstige discipline
hier bloedserieus wordt genomen.

Met de titel wordt zwaar ingezet op de emotionele lading
van het schilderij. Deze benadrukt niet alleen een dramatische
stemming, maar dwingt ook een bepaalde leesaard af. De druppel
kan niet anders begrepen worden dan als een traan. Via de traan
doemt een cartooneske menselijke gestalte op die tussen de
verfplassen en kwaststroken verschijnt. Een prozaïsch verhaal
komt te voorschijn en verdringt iedere ervaring van een zuiver
schilderkunstige uiteenzetting in de materie. Wat domineert is
het beeld van een in zichzelf gekeerde mens die zijn eigen tranen
opvangt in een open hand voorzien van een sierlijk collier.

Nadat de traan en bijbehorende figuratie is
waargenomen, is deze perceptie niet meer terug te draaien. De
schilderexpressie, de virtuoze behandeling van de materie, kan
vervolgens niet meer als onverstoord rechtstreekse esthetische
verbeelding worden ervaren. De traan lijkt daarmee ook een
toespeling op het verdriet over de ontoereikendheid van de
schilderkunst. De hand die de enkelvoudige traan opvangt, kan
worden geïnterpreteerd als een ultieme poging de schilderkunst
niet te hoeven verliezen.

—

ÉÉN KANS
JEREMIAH DAY

Waar gaat het om bij de kleinere openbaring, het
bescheiden beeld en het drama op menselijke schaal?

In een eerdere catalogus schreef Rezi van Lankveld voor
mij de opdracht: *"het kan allemaal erger!"*

De dood van het schilderen. Je hoort van die verhalen.
CalArts in de jaren tachtig, schilders die uit groepsrecensies
werden verjaagd: "En neem je behang maar met je mee!" Maar ik
ben naar de tempel van Eli Broad geweest, een torengebouw op
het strand waarin zijn collectie is ondergebracht; dit gebouw is
prachtig ingericht met werken van Hans Haacke, die onder meer
Shell bekritiseren.

Met andere woorden, wanneer het er op lijkt dat de
meest "kritische" kunstwerken prima als decoratie kunnen dienen,
dan moet zo'n werking gemeten worden in graden, zelfs in fracties.

Die schilderijen dus – ze hangen aan de muur, ze zien er mooi uit, maar zijn ze slechts decor? (Elke verdediging in woorden zou een verloren strijd zijn – hij 'doth protest too much' – dus oordeel zelf.)

De choreograaf antwoordde: "Ik geloof niet in improvisatie. Het bestaat niet. Eigenlijk is er alleen maar real-time compositie." Claims over spontaniteit, het onmiddellijke en intuïtie, zo suggereerde hij daarmee, worden overdreven; in plaats daarvan is er het opeenhopingsproces van beslissingen en uitvoering, oordeel, beslissingen en uitvoering.

Voor het geëngageerde publiek van de "real-time compositie", dat bijvoorbeeld kijkt en luistert naar Pharaoh Sanders of een andere jazzbeoefenaar, zijn we erbij voor het proces, voor de lol. Wij kunnen ook oordelen en beslissen, maar we moeten even afwachten waar de musicus heen wil, wat hij wil doen, en dan beleven we de sensatie van de verrassing, bevestiging, of ook wel teleurstelling. We zitten er niet totaal vrij van onze eigen behoeftes of problemen, maar zijn toch ook geen losgekoppelde toeschouwer. Tijdens de trompetsolo herhaalt de pianist eindeloos zijn riedel en zet zo een structuur neer van waaruit de solist kan spelen: een daad van ondersteuning. Zo functioneert onze aanwezigheid in de ruimte eveneens als ondersteuning, en misschien kunnen we zelfs het gevoel krijgen dat we iets toevoegen, door getuige te zijn, actief deel te nemen en er aandacht aan te geven.

In de tijd dat de improvisatiemuziek heel serieus werd beoefend en besproken, kregen de productie, distributie en platenverkoop een heel andere dimensie. De platen waren letterlijk alleen opnames, objecten van een boog of frase van de real-time compositie, duidelijk gedocumenteerd en via de distributie aangeboden aan "liefhebbers". *Ascension* van John Coltrane, of eerder nog *Free Jazz: A Collective Improvisation* van Ornette Coleman krijgen hun structuur vooral van hun eindpunten – *cut in, cut out* – een tijdvak van veertig minuten vastgelegd voor het nageslacht, waarbij de duur werd bepaald door de lengte van de standaard-lp. Meer nog dan de beslissingen die vallen binnen zo'n sessie zelf – met spelers die bedenken op welk moment ze op de voorgrond treden, wanneer ze weer terugtreden en plaatsmaken voor een ander, of zich zelfs helemaal inhouden, met een expliciete afwezigheid die het creëren van negatieve ruimte tot een afgewogen beslissing maakt – en meer nog dan de kwaliteit van het spelen (en vergeet niet wat voor genadeloos technisch perfectionisme deze musici zichzelf opleggen), bestaat de esthetische uitdrukking van zulke werken vooral uit de relatie tussen proces en product, het vasthouden aan het primaat van het "live"moment, met afgeronde lp's, cd's, of tegenwoordig mp3's als relicten.

In dit verband is het interessant om op te merken dat dit hoofdstuk binnen de jazz effectief werd afgesloten met *Bitches Brew* van Miles Davis. Davis brak toen met dit esthetisch principe en besloot studiotechnieken – "post-productie" – niet alleen als een documentatie-instrument in te zetten, maar ook voor actieve compositie en vakmanschap.

De parallellen tussen real-time compositie in de jazz en in het schilderen zijn dusverre te weinig betheoretiseerd en zijn ondergewaardeerd, waarschijnlijk vanwege de verschillen in sociaal milieu; hoewel sommige uitspraken van John Coltrane, over zijn wezenlijke metafysische interesses, doen denken aan beweringen van Mark Rothko of Barnett Newman, en beiden de opvatting deelden dat de esthetische praktijk de mogelijkheden biedt voor een breder effect, zo niet in de politiek dan toch op zijn minst op humanitair vlak. Maar terwijl volgende generaties en zelfs de critici van die tijd dit gedeelde esthetische ethos niet navolgden, waren de beoefenaars zelf zich hier zeer wel van bewust, zoals nog het explicietst naar voren komt in Ornette Colemans gebruik van Jackson Pollocks *White Light* voor de platenhoes van zijn album *Free Jazz*. (Het is interessant – om terug te keren naar de kwestie van het afdoen van de schilderkunst als decoratief – dat er tal van essays zijn geschreven over het gebruik van Pollocks werk als achtergrond voor *Vogue Magazine* in 1951, maar dat er slechts weinig aandacht is uitgegaan naar Colemans toe-eigening van Pollock en wat deze samenkomst zou kunnen onthullen.)

Een echo of erfenis van deze relatie tussen real-time compositie en schilderen klinkt door in de vraag die in groepsbesprekingen van schilderijen op kunstacademies soms nog wordt gehoord: "Wat denk je dat de laatste zet is geweest?" Met andere woorden, wat was de beslissende factor die maakte dat het schilderij "af" was? Want deze beslissing is van een andere orde dan de andere; dit is de beslissing die inbreekt in het proces, niet om het te onderbreken, maar om het te beëindigen en zo zijn essentiële "heelheid" te definiëren. Meer nog dan in de jazz, is de beslissing over het beëindigen van een schilderij de belangrijkste in de hiërarchie van beslissingen, omdat vanaf dat moment "het werken aan" verandert in "een werk", en een beweging in de tijd gekristalliseerd wordt in een manifestatie in de ruimte. Men "beklimt een berg omdat hij er is", en men maakt kunst "omdat het er niet is", zoals Carl Andre zei, en deze berg, die zal blijven staan voor latere generaties, zal altijd blijven galmen met de echo van deze laatste beslissing – hoe te eindigen.

Net zoals de veertigminutengrens die bovengenoemde albums definieerde, is de beslissende zet die het werk van Rezi van Lankveld bezielt en structureert het tot stand brengen van een beeld, waarna het besluit valt dat een schilderij af is.

De lange route van het doordenken van die muzikale traditie bereidt hopelijk de weg voor het beschouwen van haar praktijk.

Ze werkt nat-in-nat, met andere woorden ze werkt in en via een continu proces van betrokkenheid met het materiaal.

Haar voltooide werken zijn dezelfde episodes van spel en worsteling, artefacten opgebouwd uit compositionele besluiten,

net als het besluit wat niet te spelen, de strengheid en het
koesteren van aandacht, het voorbereidend werk, de focus op het
waken over het proces – alsof de sfeer van oordelen en timing echt
kan worden weergegeven – deze hele onzegbare substantie wordt
de belangrijkste communicatieve inhoud van haar werk.

Waar gaat het om in deze herschikking van de
traditionele rol van een proces dat uitvloeit in een product – in
het algemeen, maar ook in het werk van Van Lankveld? Donald
Judd was zo geboeid door de manier waarop een kunstwerk kon
bestaan als een relict van een beslissing, dat hij na het schrijven
over wat bekend werd als het "one shot"-schilderij (een term
die nog het meest geassocieerd wordt met Helen Frankenthaler,
Kenneth Noland, en anderen) een theorie ontwikkelde dat
zulke werken een breuk vormden met de Europese "deel/geheel,
relationele" compositie, en de volkomen rationalistische filosofie
die daarbij hoorde. Dit verwerkte hij in zijn eigen kunstwerken,
die producten waren van een enkel idee dat werd geformuleerd
door een niet-kunstzinnig proces van fabricatie, "bedenk>voer
uit". Judd beweerde groots dat zijn werk een heel nieuwe uiting
was, een meer accuraat "open" filosofisch model van de niet-
gedetermineerde ontmoeting.

Zulke ambitieuze uitspraken kunnen niet verder afstaan
van de rol van kunstenaar die Van Lankveld aanneemt. Bij haar
wordt zelfs de neiging tot heroïsme in het esthetisch gebaar
tegengegaan door het vasthouden aan wispelturigheid en een
lichte toets. Verder is Van Lankvelds praktijk, in tegenstelling tot
de hele gemeenschap van leeftijdsgenoten waar zij uit voortkomt,
compleet tegengesteld aan die van de wereldreiziger, of van de toe-
eigening van steeds grotere productiewijzen. Van Lankveld reist
zelden en is niet genegen een atelierassistent aan te nemen, zelfs
niet voor de meest routinematige klussen. Hoewel het werk geen
technische virtuositeit etaleert, is er een duidelijk engagement met
een praktijk. Net zoals John Coltrane thuis kon komen van een
optreden en daar nog een uur of twee op zijn trompet bleef spelen
– maar dan zonder echt te blazen, om de kinderen niet wakker
te maken – zo communiceert de strengheid van haar oeuvre haar
engagement met het waken over haar eigen aanpak.

Maar we gaan ons nu niet laten afleiden door enige valse
bescheidenheid; waar het om gaat in deze bredere esthetische
ethiek die duidelijk wordt gedeeld door haar praktijk, is het
problematiseren van de status van middelen en doel, handelen en
fabricatie. Mijn gebruik van deze termen komt voort uit het werk
van Hannah Arendt, waar het onderscheid wordt gemaakt tussen
werken en handelen, waarbij werken een middelen-doelrelatie
in stand houdt, en alles ondergeschikt is aan het eindproduct.
Handelen, daarentegen, is de initiatie van een onvoorspelbaar
proces. Arendt was het meest geïnteresseerd in de manieren
waarop werkprincipes naar het handelen waren verschoven, vooral
het gebruik van het motto "het doel heiligt de middelen" in de
politiek. De klassieke uitspraak van de 20ste-eeuwse politiek "men

kan geen omelet maken zonder eieren te breken" leidde tot een
respons van Arendt in haar essay "The eggs speak up." Arendts
standpunt is dat in de politiek, de arena van het handelen, de
doelen zo onvoorspelbaar zijn dat ze de middelen nooit kunnen
heiligen, en belangrijker nog, dat de middelen het doel vaak
overleven en ook een grotere invloed uitoefenen. Maar deze
lezing van de politiek als "werk", waarbij de terminologie van de
fabricatie die van het handelen ter zijde schuift, ligt niet alleen
aan de basis van het administratieve model van de meest verlichte
westerse regimes, maar ook van de machtspolitiek van minder
sympathieke staatsmachten.

Met het risico de rode draad een beetje te verliezen, kan
ik misschien toch opmerken dat, net zoals de fabricatie de politiek
heeft overgenomen, en wij in de laatste honderd jaar gewoon de
eieren zijn geworden om die omelet mee te maken, tegelijkertijd
ook de ervaring van de menselijke capaciteit tot handelen,
spontaniteit, real-time oordelen, beslissen en uitvoeren uit de
politiek verhuisd is, en kernactiviteit is geworden van allerhande
culturele praktijken. Dus toen die choreograaf het bestaan van de
"improvisatie" verwierp, ging het wellicht om belangrijker zaken
dan het technisch onderscheid, en zouden de implicaties van de
kunst als evenement een bredere betekenis kunnen hebben, en
een grotere vraag kunnen poneren. Zonder overdrijving kan het
genoeg zijn om te zeggen dat deze consideraties die werken zo'n
resonantie geven, en ons zo in hun greep houden.

**"…dit tijdperk eist niet langer een vage reactie op de
vraag 'Wat kan er gedaan worden?' …Nu gaat het er om, als we
in het nu willen blijven, om bijna wekelijks antwoord te geven
op de vraag: 'Wat gebeurt er?' "**
– Guy Debord, *brief aan Eduardo Rothe*, 1974

Het beeld. Niet slechts de structuur van de fabricatie
heeft terreinwinst geboekt in de politiek, maar daarnaast
hebben ook het georganiseerd gebruik van beeldvorming en
de aantrekkingskracht van symbolen onze publieke ruimte
getransformeerd, waardoor ieder van ons als individu onzeker is
over wat we nu zien, misschien zelfs in de spiegel, en zeker op
straat, in het parlement. De laatste tien jaar zijn zelfs de meest
vastomlijnde gelaatstrekken net zo solide als een gezicht in de
wolken.

Deze figuren die het werk van Van Lankveld bevolken
hebben meer van doen met tekenen dan met schilderen. Als
we het principe van de schets even aangrijpen, waarbij getracht
wordt met zo weinig mogelijke belijning en schaduw een figuur
of een tafereel aan te duiden, blijven deze beelden op die manier
toch onaf, hoewel ze geheel gestructureerd zijn volgens hun
relatie van proces tot afgerond werk. Of anders gezegd, hun
communicatiestijl is meer evocatief dan denotatief, en ze bieden
ons niet alleen de ruimte om ons af te vragen welke figuren vanuit

de kleinere momenten in elk schilderij naar voren zullen treden, maar verder krijgen we, zonder dat we precies weten waarom, een gevoel bij elk kenmerk van narratief en gemoedstoestand, het tafereel dat geschetst wordt door deze gezichten en meisjes en benen.

Omen of the Day – een zeldzaam landschap. Natuurlijk is er de subtekst voor de kunstenaar, maar haar terughoudendheid is verstandig. Midden in de immense zee van onwetendheid in mijn leven kunnen episodes de kwaliteit van voortekenen krijgen. Zo reed ik door het veld met een Mohawk-vrouw die met grote stelligheid beweerde dat overvliegende haviken tekens van God waren – niet positief of negatief, tekenen van geluk of ongeluk, maar een beetje zoals punctuatietekens die je moet herkennen. Het gezicht van de conducteur in de tram, plotselinge regen waar je niet aan kan ontsnappen op de fiets, de diagnose van de dokter – heb ik dagelijkse voortekenen, zoals mijn dagelijks brood?

Voorteken voor vandaag – betekenis die wordt opgeschort. De vraag van betekenis en ontvangst, herkenning en berekening wordt voor ons opgevoerd. Ons dagelijks recht, onze dagelijkse respons, misschien zelfs onze dagelijkse verantwoordelijkheid.

Een episode omlijnd door haar begin en haar eind, waarin we herkennen wat we kunnen identificeren met het gekke gezicht in de afbeelding – zoals het gezicht in de spiegel. Proces, en product. Immers, ook wij krijgen maar één kans om het goed te doen. *Hey*, het kon erger.

—

SCHRIJVENDE VUURVLIEGJES
MELISSA GRONLUND

"Absurd genoeg zijn wij gewend aan het wonder dat luttele geschreven tekens onsterfelijke beelden kunnen bevatten, en ons meenemen in het denken en naar nieuwe werelden van levende mensen die spreken, huilen, lachen. Wij beschouwen dit zo domweg als vanzelfsprekend dat we eigenlijk, juist door deze brute daad van routinematige acceptatie, het werk van eeuwen tenietdoen: de geschiedenis van de geleidelijke ontplooiing van de poëtische beschrijving en constructie, van de boommens tot Browning, van de holenmens tot Keats. Maar wat als we op een dag allemaal ontwaken en ontdekken dat we helemaal niet meer kunnen lezen?"
– Vladimir Nabokov, *Pale Fire*

In zijn casestudy *The Man Who Mistook His Wife for a Hat* vertelt dr. Oliver Sacks over iemand met prosopagnosie, een neurologische aandoening waarbij mannen en vrouwen geen gezichten kunnen herkennen, zelfs niet de gezichten van mensen uit hun naaste omgeving. Zij slagen er niet in vrienden, vrouw en kinderen te identificeren, en zijn soms zelfs niet in staat om op het meest basale niveau een persoon als zodanig te herkennen.

Zo stond de patiënt in de casestudy van Sacks bijvoorbeeld op om de dokter te begroeten, maar liep naar de staande klok en probeerde zijn hand te schudden. In het kantoor van de dokter nam hij het hoofd van zijn vrouw in zijn handen en probeerde het op zijn hoofd te zetten. Sacks zelf lijdt ook aan deze aandoening; later beschrijft hij in zijn artikel "Face Blindness" in *The New Yorker* hoe hij eens zijn baard kamde in de spiegel – tot hij erachter kwam dat die "spiegel" een andere bebaarde man was, die hem geërgerd aankeek.

Bij gevallen van prosopagnosie zijn het vooral de mensen rondom de persoon met de aandoening die getroffen worden door gevoelens van teleurstelling en irritatie. De prosopagniepatiënt zelf lopen vrolijk hun kinderen en vrienden voorbij; ze voelen soms wel een zekere gêne, maar niet het diep onbehaaglijke gevoel dat iemand zonder prosopagnosie in dergelijke omstandigheden zou voelen. Voor mensen met prosopagnosie is dit gebrek aan herkenning net zo normaal als het niet kunnen lezen van een vreemd schrift. Maar voor diegenen die in alle talen toch een zekere leesbaarheid zien, is het niet kunnen onderscheiden van mensen angstaanjagend, omdat het niet alleen een perceptueel, maar ook een cognitief defect impliceert. Het is het falen van begrip en geheugen, twee bastions van waaruit een gevoel van zelfbewustzijn wordt gevormd.

De schilderijen van Rezi van Lankveld betreden dit emotioneel en psychologisch beladen veld – met hun gezichten, vormen en structuren die ternauwernood uit het schilderwerk opdoemen. Haar figuren zweven op de rand van herkenbaarheid en voeren daar de vraag op hoe men elementen kan onderscheiden en zich kan oriënteren op de wereld – en roepen de bevrediging en verrassing van de herkenning op, maar ook de frustratie en de verwarring van alleen maar vormen en kleuren zien. In de beginperiode van het modernisme, in de vroeg-20ste eeuw, waren de psychologische implicaties van de overgang van representatie naar abstractie onderwerp van een levendig debat: zo is alom bekend dat Erwin Panofsky, maar ook anderen, naar abstractie keken om te begrijpen hoe het oog en het brein vormen naar herkenbare figuren vertalen, met andere woorden, hoe het brein gaten in de informatie tracht op te heffen om een "figuur" te zien, of hoe het een beroep doet op geleerd geheugen om een soort relatie te "begrijpen", bijvoorbeeld een moeder-zoonrelatie, terwijl er in wezen slechts vormen te zien zijn. Deze discussie wordt door de dubbelzinnige beelden van Van Lankveld nieuw leven ingeblazen, maar de aandacht gaat uit naar hun procesmatige kwaliteiten: hoe verloopt het proces van deze herkenning, en, wellicht nog belangrijker, met welke affectieve dimensie gaat dit gepaard?

Bij het doorgronden van dit probleem zouden we twee temporaliteiten van kijken kunnen identificeren, hand in hand met de net genoemde schildercategorieën: de lange duur van het waarderen en begrijpen van een werk, waarvan de betekenis wordt overgebracht met steun van verschillende vormen en gestaltes, en daarnaast de onmiddellijke herkenning van een scène. Van Lankvelds werk beweegt zich tussen beide; bij haar komt dat tweede als een schok, niet slechts een schok van herkenning, maar de verrassing dat het schilderij dat we dachten te kennen – namelijk dat werk dat ging over textuur, kleur en vorm – in feite stiekem naar ons terugkeek, en ons zo een uitzicht bood waarin wij zelf ook gesitueerd konden worden. Want als abstractie een visuele uitgestrektheid suggereert, dan bouwt representatie aan een veld voor het menselijk subject, dat de vormen voor hem of haar herkent als blijken van een wereld waarin hij of zij zou kunnen bestaan.

Dit is opzettelijk niet scherp omlijnd in het werk van Van Lankveld, omdat zij zowel het feit als de daad van herkenning problematiseert. In *Hero* (2010) staren twee ogen en een mond onzeker vanuit hun verfomhulling naar buiten; de contouren van een lichaam kijken in *Hij kijkt naar jou* (2010) naar de kijker, zoals de titel suggereert, of kijken misschien over zijn schouder – of wellicht bestaan ze helemaal niet. In *Omen of the Day* (2009) prijkt een klein stadje, bestaande uit een toren en een groep gebouwen, onwaarschijnlijk boven op een golf van pure verf. Kunnen we er zeker van zijn dat we ook echt iets zien – is het een truc van de verf, gezichtsbedrog van de olie, of zelfs een foefje dat ons uit de abstractie trekt? Hoewel haar werk figuren creëert, lijken deze eerder te behoren tot de verf dan tot een menselijke beeldtaal; en het vermogen deze figuren te herkennen maakt ze niet geschikt voor een figuratieve scène, maar eerder voor een narratief dat stamt uit haar proces – van hoe ze de werken maakte en op welke manier, of wanneer, ze stopte.

Deze performativiteit doet weer denken aan een curieus aspect van Sacks' verhaal over de man die zijn vrouw aanzag voor een hoed. De man in kwestie was een musicoloog, die zijn vermogen om gezichten en nuttige objecten te herkennen als het ware inruilde voor de muziek als ordeningsprincipe voor de dagelijkse routine: als hij zong of neuriede, kon hij zonder problemen een maaltijd eten. Als hij stopte met zingen, keek hij in verwarring naar de vork in zijn hand, of naar de mensen tegenover hem. Wanneer hij dan weer begon te neuriën, gaven de vrij zwevende vormen en gestaltes weer hun functie aan hem prijs, en kon hij weer verdergaan met het gebruiken van het bestek en een gesprekje voeren met zijn vrouw en vrienden aan tafel. Bij het verslechteren van zijn toestand bleef hij bijna continu neuriën of pianospelen, waarbij hij vrijwel totaal vertrouwde op de interne logica of sensibiliteit van de muziek om zijn dag begrijpelijk te maken, wat voorheen via de visuele herkenning gebeurde.

Door het inruilen van één zintuig (zien) voor een ander (horen), heeft neuriën het effect dat het de daad van het kijken zichtbaar maakt – ofwel, zoals bij deze patiënt, wordt kijken vervangen door een ander zintuiglijk proces. (Sommige, met name vroegere werken van Van Lankveld lijken zich ook bezig te houden met het direct in kaart brengen van deze aandacht of dit proces, vooral door de driedimensionale indruk die ze wekken. (In werken zoals *Grey Man* [2009] en de reeks ongetitelde werken uit de periode 2001-2003, is verf op verf opgebracht om elke figuur te schilderen, zodat de schilderijen in materieel opzicht – dus niet alleen representatief – grafieken zijn die plekken van activiteit aanduiden.) Met andere woorden, neurieën dramatiseert de daad van het waarnemen, en verandert een resultaat ("ik zie iemand!") in een proces, een daad.

Je zou deze fluïde sensibiliteit, of hoe kijken zich vermengt met muziek en beweging, kunnen plaatsen naast de gruwel die wordt opgeroepen door de verteller in het hierboven geciteerde fragment uit Nabokovs *Pale Fire:* die is bang dat hij niet meer in staat zal zijn de balpenaantekeningen op zijn notitiekaarten te ontcijferen, maar uiteindelijk verwisselt hij deze dystopie toch voor de torenhoge hoop op een soort superleesbaarheid – dat je bijvoorbeeld zou kunnen decoderen hoe vuurvliegjes 'signalen van gestrande geesten' in de 'gekneusde en gehavende nachtlucht' schrijven. Dit performatief begrijpen vat herkenning op als een altijd procesmatige daad, waarbij de herkenning niet binair is (ja, ik zie het/nee, ik zie het niet) en die het schilderen ver wegstuurt van het moeten representeren of repliceren. Van Lankvelds werken participeren in een breder discours van "het kijken" – iets wat door veel hedendaagse schilders wordt verkend. Dit doet ze niet door te focusen op de machtspolitiek van de blik, maar door het kijkproces zowel emotioneel als psychologisch op losse schroeven te zetten. Als we niet weten hoe we zien, hoe kunnen we dan zeker weten wat we zien? Of zijn er andere manieren om met schilderijen om te gaan – bijvoorbeeld performatief, net als bij de neuriënde prosopagnosiepatiënt, of onbepaald, een uitgedijde horizon die nooit gesloten is of in context gebracht? Door de representativiteit te isoleren zodat deze niet langer een ijkpunt kan zijn – haar schilderijen zijn geen landschappen of portretten – zoomt Van Lankveld bovendien in op de kwestie van de herkenbaarheid zelf, de unieke band daarvan met de schilderkunst, die als historische taak had dingen te creëren die we wel of niet herkennen als lijkend op iets anders.

Maar als we te veel concentreren op de figuren, veronachtzamen we hun achtergrond: de gekneusde en gehavende luchten van de niet-herkenning die achter de vormen zweven, in een tweedimensionale niet-ruimte. De sterk affectieve waarde van deze kleuren en vormen toont misschien de angst voor het niet-representatieve, maar ook de vreugde ervan: alternatieve manieren van denken, om in te bewegen en om de wereld te zien, die een directere band aangaan met de emoties van de kijker dan met zijn of haar cognitieve begrip. Laten we prosopagnosie niet als een vloek beschouwen, maar als een kans.

REZI VAN LANKVELD
Born *Geboren* 1973, Almelo

EDUCATION
OPLEIDING

1997–1999
— Jan van Eyck Academie, Maastricht

1993–1997
— Gerrit Rietveld Academie, Amsterdam

SOLO EXHIBITIONS
SOLOTENTOONSTELLINGEN

2010
— Friedrich Petzel Gallery, New York
— The Approach, London

2008
— *Paintings on Paper*, The Approach W1, London

2007
— Friedrich Petzel Gallery, New York

2005
— The Approach, London
— Galerie Diana Stigter, Amsterdam

2003
— The Approach, London

2002
— Loerakker Galerie, Amsterdam

GROUP EXHIBITIONS
GROEPSTENTOONSTELLINGEN

2011
— *Rue Julien Dulait*, Charleroi
   Curated by Gert Robijns

2009
— *Christopher Orr & J. Parker Valentine & Rezi van Lankveld*, The Front Room, Contemporary Art Museum St. Louis
— *The Clotted Body*, Rezi van Lankveld & Tim Stoner, Galerie Diana Stigter, Amsterdam
— *Being There*, Galerie Akinci, Amsterdam

2008
— *Back to black, the color black in current painting*, Kestnergesellschaft, Hanover
— *Paintings: 1936–2008*, The Approach W1, London

2007
— *Salon Nouveau*, Engleholm Englehorn Galerie, Vienna
— *Accidental Painting*, Perry Rubenstein Gallery, New York

2006–2007
— *Le Nouveau Siècle*, Museum Van Loon, Amsterdam
— *Schilderkunst Nederland - Deutschland Malerei*, GEM, museum voor actuele kunst, The Hague

2005
— Museum Kunst Palast, Düsseldorf
— *Interested Painting*, Gallery 400, University of Chicago, Illinois

2004
— *Her Kind*, The Approach, London

2003
— Galerie Diana Stigter, Amsterdam
— *Dirty Pictures*, The Approach, London

2002
— *Free space*, Hasselt, Belgium

2001
— *Royal Prize / Koninklijke Subsidie*, Gemeentemuseum Den Haag, The Hague

2000
— *Atopie*, Hedah, Maastricht

1999
— *Free space*, NICC, Antwerp

BIBLIOGRAPHY
BIBLIOGRAFIE

2008
— Goodling, Francis, "Critic's Choice: Rezi van Lankveld", *Time Out London*, 14–20 August 2008, No. 1982

2007
— Weich, John, "Future Greats: Rezi van Lankveld", *Art Review*, March, Issue 09, pp. 93

2006
— Ribas, João, "Emerging Artists", *Art+Auction*, May, Vol. XXIX No. 9, pp. 128–129 (illus.)

2005
— Gronlund, Melissa, "Rezi van Lankveld", *Frieze*, May, Issue 91
— Hubbard, Sue, "Rezi van Lankveld@ The Approach", *The Independent*,
— Herbert, Martin, "Rezi van Lankveld", *Artforum*, Summer, pp. 339–340

2003
— Bell, Eugina, "Rezi van Lankveld", *Artforum.com*, 2nd April
— Higgie, Jennifer, "Rezi van Lankveld", *Frieze*, Issue 78, October
— Herbert, Martin, "Rezi van Lankveld", *Tema Celeste*, No. 99
— O'Reilly, Sally, "Rezi van Lankveld", *Time Out*, No. 1718, 23–30 July
— Falconer, Morgan, "Rezi van Lankveld / The Approach", *What's On in London*, 23–30 July

WORKS / **WERKEN**

p. 11
SPIRIT, **2009**
Oil on canvas
160 x 132 cm / 62.9 x 51.8 in
Courtesy Friedrich Petzel Gallery, New York

p. 21
UNTITLED, **2003**
Oil on board
27 x 31 cm / 10.6 x 12.2 in
Collection Drosterij/Knispel, Amsterdam

p. 22
SECOND NATURE, **2004**
Oil on board
122 x 122 cm / 48 x 48 in
Collection University of Chicago Booth School of Business, Chicago

p. 29
OLD PLANET, **2009**
Oil on canvas
130 x 130 / 51.18 x 51.18 in
Collection De Bruin-Heijn

p. 31
SPREAD, **2004**
Oil on board
43 x 60 cm / 16.9 x 23.6 in
Advaney Collection

p. 33
DREAM DREAM, **2003**
Oil on board
46 x 47.5 / 18.1 x 18.7 in

p. 36
EGO (DEGAS), **2006**
Oil on board
151 x 99 cm / 59.4 x 39 in
Collection the artist

p. 39
IDEAS OF SOLUTION, **2005**
Oil on board
152 x 151.5 cm / 59.8 x 59.6 in
Private Collection, London

p. 41
SOUVENIR, **2005**
Oil on board
122.5 x 121.5 cm / 48.2 x 47.8 in
Collection Igor DaCosta, New York

p. 43
DISPOSSESSION, **2006**
Oil on board
122 x 122 cm / 48 x 48 in
Collection Babak Eftekhari, London

p. 51
TEARS, **2009**
Oil on canvas
120 x 120 cm / 47.24 x 47.24 in
Courtesy Friedrich Petzel Gallery, New York

p. 53
LISTEN, **2007**
Oil on board
63 x 60 cm / 24.8 x 23.6 in
Private Collection, New York

p. 55
A MON SEUL DÉSIR, **2006**
Oil on board
122 x 122 cm / 48 x 48 in
Collection Laura Steinberg & Bernardo Nadal-Ginard, Boston

p. 57
LITTLE BLUE RAPE, **2006**
Oil on board
32 x 35 cm / 12.6 x 13.8 in
Collection Laura Steinberg & Bernardo Nadal-Ginard, Boston

p. 59
THERE WAS A YOUNG LADY FROM HELL WHO JUMPED AT THE SOUND OF A BELL BECAUSE SHE WAS BAD-BAD-BAD, **2007**
Oil on board
135 x 121.5 / 53.1 x 47.8 in
Collection De Bruin-Heijn

p. 61
ROCK, **2007**
Oil on board
120 x 120 cm / 47.2 x 47.2 in
Collection Leslie and Michael Weissman, Courtesy of BaliMillerInc

p. 62
NERVES, **2007**
Oil on board
66 x 62 cm / 26 x 24.4 in
Collection Honor Fraser and Stavros Merjos

p. 71
OMEN OF THE DAY, **2009**
Oil on canvas
60 x 50 cm / 25.59 x 19.69 in
Collection Leslie and Michael Weissman, Courtesy of BaliMillerInc

p. 73
SUBURBIA, **2009**
Oil on canvas
125 x 110 cm / 49.21 x 43.31 in
Courtesy Friedrich Petzel Gallery, New York

p. 75
UNTITLED (SPILLIAERT), **2009**
Oil on board
31 x 27 cm / 12.2 x 10.6 in
Cobra to Contemporary, collection Hugo and Carla Brown

p. 76
NEST, **2009**
Oil on canvas
60 x 50 cm, 23.62 x 19.69 in
Courtesy Friedrich Petzel Gallery, New York

p. 79
MISI MOISY, **2009**
Oil on canvas
65 x 50 cm / 25.59 x 19.69 in
Collection David Madee

p. 81
SWAN, **2009**
Oil on canvas
40 x 30 cm / 15.75 x 11.81 in
Collection Harm and Floor Haak, The Netherlands

p. 83
XXXXXX, **2009**
Oil on canvas
125 x 110 cm / 49.21 x 43. 31 in
Courtesy Friedrich Petzel Gallery, New York

p. 85
LAZILY FAIRY, **2010**
Oil on canvas
60 x 50 cm / 23.6 x 19.7 in
Collection Aedes Real Estate, Amsterdam

p. 87
HIJ KIJKT NAAR JOU, **2010**
Oil on canvas
80 x 70 cm / 31.5 x 27.6 in
Private Collection, London

p. 89
ON THE PRAIRIE, **2010**
Oil on canvas
120 x 120 cm / 47.2 x 47.2 in
Collection Schulp-Janssen, Amsterdam

p. 91
CANNES, **2010**
Oil on canvas
105 x 90 cm / 41.3 x 35.4 in
Collection David Roberts, London

p. 92
HERO, **2010**
Oil on canvas
125 x 110 cm, 49.21 x 43.31 in
Courtesy Friedrich Petzel Gallery, New York

p. 97
SYMPTOM, **2010**
Oil on canvas
135 x 120 cm / 53.1 x 47.2 in
Courtesy The Approach, London

p. 100
MOUNTAIN OF ZORRO, **2010**
Oil on canvas
80 x 56 cm / 31.5 x 22 in
Courtesy Schulp-Janssen, Amsterdam

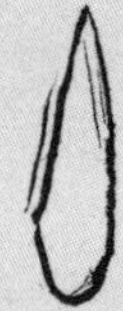
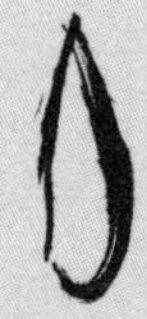
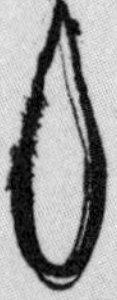
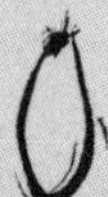

COLOPHON / **COLOFON**

Texts *Teksten*
Jeremiah Day
Leen Bedaux
Melissa Gronlund
Zlatko Wurzberg

Translation *Vertaling*
Dorrie Tattersall (NL-ENG / ENG-NL)
Vlatka Valentić (KR-ENG)

Final editing *Eindredactie*
Els Brinkman

Graphic Design *Grafisch Ontwerp*
Roosje Klap, Amsterdam
WWW.ROOSJEKLAP.NL

Photos *Fotografie*
Edo Kuipers
FXP, London
Gert Jan van Rooij
Larry Lamay
Linelle Deunk (p. 8)

Printing *Druk*
Calff & Meischke, Amsterdam

Binding *Binder*
Van Waarden, Zaandam

Paper *Papier*
Arco Print 100 gsm
Revive 125 gsm
Chromolux 100 gsm
Satogami 116 gsm (cover)

© 2011 all artworks
Rezi van Lankveld

WWW.THEAPPROACH.CO.UK

ISBN 978 1 905464 50 0

All rights reserved.

No part of this publication may be reproduced or transmitted in any form or by any means, electronic or mechanical, including photocopy, recording or any information storage and retrieval system, without permission in writing from the copyright owners.

This publication was made possible through the generous contribution of the Fonds BKVB.

Special thanks to *Speciale dank aan*
Paul van Esch, Zlatko Wurzberg, Leen Bedaux, Hartmut Wilkening, Jeremiah Day, Alisa Margolis, Bedep Tran, Yixue Wu, Arjan van Helmond, Roosje Klap, Antoine Bertaudière, Freek Kuin, Delphine Bedel, Jake Miller, The Approach Gallery, Friedrich Petzel, Andrea Teschke.

Ridinghouse Publisher
Doro Globus

Ridinghouse
5-8 Lower John Street
Golden Square
London W1F 9DR
United Kingdom
WWW.RIDINGHOUSE.CO.UK

Distributed in the UK and Europe by
Cornerhouse
70 Oxford Street
Manchester M1 5NH
United Kingdom
WWW.CORNERHOUSE.ORG

Distributed in the US by
RAM Publications
2525 Michigan Avenue Building A2
Santa Monica CA 90404
United States
WWW.RAMPUB.COM

All rights reserved.
No part of this book may be reproduced or transmitted in any form or by any means, electronic or mechanical, including photocopying, recording or any other information storage or retrieval system, without prior permission in writing from the publisher.

British Library Cataloguing-in-Publication Data. A full catalogue record of this book is available from the British Library

For the book in this form
© Ridinghouse

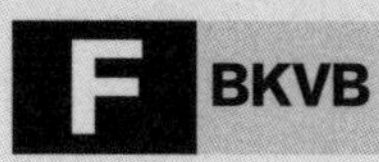